Max Planck Institute for Innovation and Competition

For further volumes/weitere Bände:
http://www.springer.com/series/7760

MPI Studies on Intellectual Property and Competition Law

Volume 23

Edited by

Josef Drexl
Reto M. Hilty
Joseph Straus

Gintarė Surblytė
Editor

Competition on the Internet

 Springer

Editor
Gintarė Surblytė
Max Planck Institute for Innovation and Competition
Munich
Germany

ISSN 2191-5822　　　　　　ISSN 2191-5830 (electronic)
ISBN 978-3-642-55095-9　　ISBN 978-3-642-55096-6 (eBook)
DOI 10.1007/978-3-642-55096-6
Springer Heidelberg New York Dordrecht London

Library of Congress Control Number: 2014949202

© Springer-Verlag Berlin Heidelberg 2015
This work is subject to copyright. All rights are reserved by the Publisher, whether the whole or part of the material is concerned, specifically the rights of translation, reprinting, reuse of illustrations, recitation, broadcasting, reproduction on microfilms or in any other physical way, and transmission or information storage and retrieval, electronic adaptation, computer software, or by similar or dissimilar methodology now known or hereafter developed. Exempted from this legal reservation are brief excerpts in connection with reviews or scholarly analysis or material supplied specifically for the purpose of being entered and executed on a computer system, for exclusive use by the purchaser of the work. Duplication of this publication or parts thereof is permitted only under the provisions of the Copyright Law of the Publisher's location, in its current version, and permission for use must always be obtained from Springer. Permissions for use may be obtained through RightsLink at the Copyright Clearance Center. Violations are liable to prosecution under the respective Copyright Law.
The use of general descriptive names, registered names, trademarks, service marks, etc. in this publication does not imply, even in the absence of a specific statement, that such names are exempt from the relevant protective laws and regulations and therefore free for general use.
While the advice and information in this book are believed to be true and accurate at the date of publication, neither the authors nor the editors nor the publisher can accept any legal responsibility for any errors or omissions that may be made. The publisher makes no warranty, express or implied, with respect to the material contained herein.

Printed on acid-free paper

Springer is part of Springer Science+Business Media (www.springer.com)

Contents

Introductory Remarks 1
Gintarė Surblytė

**Selective Distribution and the Internet: Lessons from Case
C-439/09** *Pierre Fabre Dermo-Cosmétique* **(13 October 2011)** 5
Stefan Enchelmaier

**Internet Competition and E-Books: Challenging the Competition
Policy** *Acquis***?** 25
Simonetta Vezzoso

A Note on Price-Parity Clauses in Platform Markets 41
Sebastian Wismer

**FTC v. Google: The Enforcement of Antitrust Law in Online
Markets** 53
Ronny Hauck

Discriminatory Conduct in the ICT Sector: A Legal Framework 63
Pablo Ibáñez Colomo

**Competition Concerns in Multi-Sided Markets in Mobile
Communication** 81
Jonas Severin Frank

**The More Technological Approach: Competition Law in the
Digital Economy** 101
Rupprecht Podszun

About the Authors

Stefan Enchelmaier studied law, philosophy, and Latin in Cologne, Hamburg, and Edinburgh; he obtained his doctorate from the University of Bonn with a thesis on European competition law and his habilitation from Ludwig-Maximilians-Universität München with a thesis on comparative Anglo-German personal property law. He held posts at the Universities of Oxford and York as well as at the Max Planck Institute for Intellectual Property and Competition Law before returning, as Professor of European and Comparative Law, to the Faculty of Law, University of Oxford, combined with a fellowship at Lincoln College, Oxford.

Jonas Severin Frank is a Research and Teaching Assistant and Doctoral Candidate at the chair of Economic Policy of Philipps-Universität Marburg. In Marburg he studied economics and currently conducts research in the areas of competition policy and the intersection of innovation and intellectual property rights. He is particularly interested in the assessment of horizontal agreements involving intellectual property as well as vertical restraints in different industries. He took part in the 5th Annual International Workshop of the European Commission—Joint Research Centre Institute for Prospective Technological Studies in Seville, Spain, and the Competition and Innovation Summer School in Turunc, Turkey. Also, he was a Visiting Research Fellow at the Ritsumeikan Asia Pacific University in Beppu, Japan.

Ronny Hauck studied at Friedrich-Alexander-Universität Erlangen-Nürnberg (FAU) (First State Examination 2004), after which he worked as associate to Professor Winfried Veelken at FAU and to Professor Christoph Ann at TU München. He passed the German bar exam in 2008. Ronny Hauck earned his doctor of laws (Dr. iur.) from the University of Augsburg in 2008, and then worked as an attorney-at-law. In 2009, he joined the faculty at TU München as a Lecturer (Akademischer Rat); there he teaches courses in antitrust and unfair competition law. In 2014, he completed his habilitation at the University of Augsburg. His research focuses on antitrust and unfair competition law as well as on IP law; he has written several books, book contributions, and law journal articles in these areas. Ronny Hauck has received multiple awards, including DAAD doctoral and post-doctoral scholarships. He was invited by the Stetson University School of Law (2007–2008) and the George Washington University Law School (2012–2013) to serve as a visiting scholar.

Pablo Ibáñez Colomo is Associate Professor of Law at the London School of Economics and Political Science. After taking an LL.M. in 2004 at the Law Department of the College of Europe (Bruges), where he then taught for 3 years, he joined the European University Institute as a Researcher in 2007, receiving his Ph.D. in June 2010 (Jacques Lassier Prize). In 2008, he spent 6 months as a TTLF fellow at Stanford Law School. He has been invited to give guest lectures at several institutions.

Rupprecht Podszun is Professor for Civil Law, Intellectual Property and Economic Law at the University of Bayreuth. He is also Co-Director of the University's Research Centre for Economic and Media Law. Rupprecht Podszun is an Affiliated Research Fellow with the Max Planck Institute for Innovation and Competition in Munich, where he worked from 2007 until 2012 as a Senior Researcher. In 2003, he completed his Ph.D. at Ludwig-Maximilians-Universität München, under the supervision of Prof. Dr. Josef Drexl with a thesis on international competition law. From 2005 to 2007 he worked as a case handler at the Bundeskartellamt, the German competition authority. In 2012, he completed his habilitation at Ludwig-Maximilians-Universität München. Rupprecht Podszun is an Individual Member of the Asian Competition Law and Economics Centre, Hong Kong, and a member of the Steering Committee and of the Board of ASCOLA, the Academic Society for Competition Law.

Gintarė Surblytė is a senior research fellow at the Max Planck Institute for Innovation and Competition (former Max Planck Institute for Intellectual Property and Competition Law) in Munich, where she conducts research in the field of competition law with a specific focus on the interface of competition and intellectual property law. In 2011 she finished her Ph.D. studies (*summa cum laude*) at Ludwig-Maximilians-Universität München supported by the scholarship from the Max Planck Institute for Intellectual Property and Competition Law. Gintarė Surblytė studied law at Vilnius University in Lithuania and also holds an LL.M. degree, which she obtained from Ludwig-Maximilians-Universität München in 2007.

Simonetta Vezzoso is a graduate of the State University of Milan Law School and she holds a Ph.D. in Economics from Witten-Herdecke-Universität in Germany. After graduation she went into private practice in Milan with the Ardito Law Office where she focused on International and Commercial Law. She is Senior Research Fellow and Professor of Intellectual Property and Competition Law at the University of Trento, Department of Economics and Management. She is a Non-Governmental Advisor to the International Competition Network, and she represents the Italian Libraries Association before the World Intellectual Property Organization. Simonetta Vezzoso has written extensively on topics in the field of competition policy and intellectual property law including vertical restraints from the perspective of evolutionary economics, abuses of dominance in technological markets, merger policy and open source, E-learning, and copyright law.

Sebastian Wismer studied mathematical economics at the University of Würzburg and wrote his dissertation in the field of industrial organization within the Bavarian Graduate Program in Economics. During his time as a research assistant at the Department of Economics (University of Würzburg) his research interests comprised the economics of vertical structures and intermediated markets. His research includes several game-theoretic models of Internet platforms, analyzing implications of specific tariff systems and vertical restraints. As a member of the interdisciplinary research group "price-based exclusionary conduct" he concentrated on current issues in competition policy. In 2013, Sebastian Wismer started working for the Federal Cartel Office (Bundeskartellamt).

Introductory Remarks

Gintarė Surblytė

Enormous as they are, the gains that appeared with the emergence of the Internet have unavoidably been confronted with constantly arising new challenges. Besides others are the issues related to competition on the Internet. The growing digital industries offer platforms which open the gates for new ways of trading, marketing, developing business and last, but not least, for competing. Yet, the Internet may be blurring the trading borders, but it should not be restricting competition. Quite to the contrary, a digital environment should promote competition, not distort it. Platforms that act as intermediaries are, on the one hand, good for that purpose. Yet, on the other hand, competition on the Internet takes place in the industries featured by network effects, rendering the so-called "platform competition" a complex and thus not a one-sided concept.

Competition begins with a market. Yet, markets in network and platform-based industries are no longer one-sided: instead they are two- or even multi-sided. With different business models and strategies involved, competition law analysis becomes complex at the very first step: market definition. The latter is challenged by the ever-emerging new tools (e.g. a market for search engines?), by the swift development of existing products (e.g. a market for operating systems?), and by the unpredictability of completely new technologies. Thus, how should the relevant market be defined in a digital environment? Might the specific features of these industries also impact the assessment of market power? To what extent do the market structure and the level of concentration matter for platform competition? Furthermore, a web-based platform acts as an intermediary between different groups of customers and consumers. This raises the question of barriers to market entry and access to a platform. Should competition authorities step in due to the threat of anti-competitive foreclosure of markets? When does the conduct of a

---

G. Surblytė (✉)
Max Planck Institute for Innovation and Competition, Munich, Germany
e-mail: Gintare.Surblyte@ip.mpg.de

dominant market player stop being drastic competition and become anti-competitive behaviour?

Time and again, competition law enforcers have been challenged by the assessment of mergers in traditional business environments. The challenges involved seem to be even greater in light of platform competition: are competition authorities up to the task and do they have the right tools for the assessment of mergers in digital industries which, due to their dynamic effects, are often even more unpredictable? Does this, on the one hand, suggest that more economic thinking should be integrated into a competition law analysis, and does this, on the other hand, raise the question of how competition authorities—which are still not equipped with "a crystal ball"—will cope with that?

Finally, the Internet is meant to be open to all. In which relation does this stand to the on-going debate on network neutrality? Might open Internet and open markets foster competition not only in terms of price, but also in terms of innovation? In dynamic industries innovation is not meant to be developed merely step-by-step, but is rather growing by way of leapfrogging (e.g. the incumbent technology). In light of such industrial developments, it is the traditional competition law concepts that may need to be developed in the first place—importantly, at industry's pace. In fact, new business models and strategies adopted in network and platform-based industries influence a competition law analysis in terms of both legal and economic thinking. How should competition law deal with the emerging and unpredictable challenges of growing digital industries? Will a constantly and swiftly developing business environment trigger a change in competition law and does this, after all, mean that time of change has come?

These questions were raised and discussed in the Post-Doc conference titled "Competition on the Internet" organized in February, 2013, in Munich. As the title of the conference indicates, the forum focused on competition law issues in a digital environment. A dynamic nature of the latter often triggers the question of whether competition law concerns that arise on the Internet are so specific that they presuppose a reconsideration of competition law concepts and their application. Current competition law tools might on the one hand be considered sufficient to tackle competition law issues arising in the digital economy. Yet, on the other hand, the question is whether these tools can or should be adjusted to the pace of dynamic industries? To what extent could competition law be supplemented by regulation—is the latter a foe or rather an ally? Given the complexity of competitive process in platform-based industries and the unpredictability in terms of innovation, it is hardly sufficient to assess the issues arising online only from the legal perspective. Just as important is an economic way of thinking in order to understand the functioning of digital industries, the markets and thus the competitive process which takes place in them. Bearing this in mind, the speakers of the conference were both lawyers and economists, so that the legal academic discussion was neatly supplemented by economic comments. The same purpose is maintained in this book, which provides an assessment of platform competition issues from a legal as well as an economic point of view. It gives an analysis of recent developments in the most relevant competition law cases in a digital environment on both sides of the Atlantic (the EU and the US).

Seizing this opportunity, I would like to thank the speakers for their talks and a highly interesting discussion during the conference as well as for their written contributions which have found their place in this book. I am grateful to Professor Dr. Josef Drexl, LL.M. (Berkeley) for his trust in me to organize the conference. I am thankful to Dr. Mor Bakhoum, LL.M. (Lausanne), LL.M. (Chicago-Kent) for his kind assistance in organizational and conceptual arrangements of the conference, to Delia Zirilli for her help in administrative matters and to Allison Felmy for her language editing support. Last, but not least, I thank the Springer Verlag for publishing this book.

Selective Distribution and the Internet: Lessons from Case C-439/09 *Pierre Fabre Dermo-Cosmétique* (13 October 2011)

Stefan Enchelmaier

Abstract In Pierre Fabre, a system of selective distribution for cosmetics was in issue which demanded that sales be made exclusively in a marked, specially allocated outlet and in the presence of a qualified pharmacist. Addressing the question whether the prohibition of internet sales pursued a legitimate aim and did so in a proportionate manner, the Court emphasised that the aim of maintaining a prestigious image was not a legitimate aim for restricting competition. The case *Copad v Dior*, by contrast, arose from a licensing agreement between a brand owner and a contract manufacturer which specifically prohibited the manufacturer from selling to discount stores. The Court held that the quality of luxury goods was not just the result of their material characteristics, but also of the allure and prestigious image which bestowed on them an aura of luxury. Therefore, impairment of that aura was likely to affect the actual quality of those goods. Crucially, this meant that no exhaustion occurred with regard to these goods under Articles 7(1) and 8(2) of the Trade Marks Directive. Despite their differences, these two cases address similar questions in incompatible ways. Stefan Enchelmaier shows that the Court's approach in *Pierre Fabre* is preferable.

1 Introduction

One of the central concepts of competition law is efficiency: competition is, generally speaking, a more efficient way of organising the production of goods and services than central planning. What is more, that competitor is the most efficient who produces the greatest output with the smallest input. The goods and

---

S. Enchelmaier (✉)
Faculty of Law, Lincoln College, University of Oxford, Oxford, UK
e-mail: stefan.enchelmaier@law.ox.ac.uk

services thus produced are then offered on markets. To these, in turn, the concept of efficiency also applies: a market is the more efficient, the better it allows supply and demand to be matched. In other words, an efficient market enables the greatest number of consumers to find suppliers of the goods and services they seek with the smallest effort and at the lowest price.

Efficiency is not a question of "either/or" but of "more or less". In reality, markets are not perfectly efficient. They are beset with inefficiencies. One such imperfection is a lack of transparency, that is, difficulty in obtaining relevant information expeditiously or at all. The internet, however, has greatly improved market transparency. The information available on the world-wide web is accessible from anywhere, anytime, and in practically unlimited quantity. Powerful search engines allow focussed enquiries, and reduce waste in time and effort. With the availability of information for consumers, the geographical scope of the markets has expanded. This is true of those markets which are not affected by prohibitive transport costs or state intervention in the form of (in EU parlance) quantitative restrictions or measures having equivalent effect (Articles 34, 35 TFEU). Language barriers and (to a decreasing extent) differences in the national systems of private law also contribute to the continued existence of separate markets as between Member States. Most importantly for present purposes, so do anti-competitive practices, whether legal or not.

All the same, many producers and distributors have seised the opportunities offered by the internet, by running dedicated online shops. Some distributors, most prominently Amazon, maintain no brick-and-mortar outlets at all. This is also true of eBay. This started as an auction platform but for a while has also enabled straightforward purchases from vendors who carry on at least part of their activities electronically. In relative terms, however, these are still fringe phenomena, if steadily growing.[1] Although traditional shops may be struggling in some markets (most notably in the sale of recorded music), this method of distribution is by no means defunct. Enough consumers are looking for what a few clicks on a computer screen cannot offer: they are looking for a shopping "experience".

This is where selective distribution comes in. It is aimed at creating an exclusive shopping atmosphere in which the products appear particularly desirable. By frequenting such shops, consumers can signal to others that they want to be seen, and can afford, to be associated with those goods and their luxurious retail surroundings. In other words, selective distribution confers status on both distributors and consumers.

Nevertheless, the décor of a shop may be particularly sumptuous, the personnel particularly well turned-out or knowledgeable, and the choice of goods particularly exquisite: it cannot escape consumers' notice that these goods can as well be sold in more humble surroundings and at considerably reduced prices. "Parallel" traders amply demonstrate this. These are economic operators outside the producers'

---

[1] See the figures reported by *Robertson*, Online sales under the Commission's Block Exemption Regulation on vertical agreements, Part 1, (2012) 33 ECLR 132, 132 ff.

"official" distribution networks who manage to obtain from insiders or from consumers quantities of goods subject to selective distribution. The parallel traders then sell these goods more cheaply, albeit in less appealing outlets and/or with fewer free services before and after sale, than the officially selected retailers.

Here again, the internet comes into focus. Online distribution drastically reduces the overhead costs associated with the transport and storage of goods. Posting from a big and automated warehouse, without access by the public and on an industrial estate by the motorway, is much cheaper per unit than selling to customers who come to a small outlet in a pedestrian zone in the centre of town. Conversely, the rationalisation to be had from online distribution allows higher margins even at lower prices. This makes online distribution especially appealing for retailers that are members of a selective distribution system. By selling their goods online, too, they can increase their turnover and thus better recoup the expense of maintaining the authorised physical outlet. This will be the case even where those retailers do not set up a dedicated warehouse elsewhere, but send all goods ordered online from their existing premises.

Such online activities, however, can create legal problems. Selective distribution pivots on physical outlets whose location, presentation, and staff meet the manufacturer's conditions for admission to its distribution system. As a consequence of these conditions the number of outlets within a given geographical area will always remain limited: not all locations are suitable, not every retailer is willing to shoulder the costs of meeting the requirements. This de facto territorial exclusivity allows the selected retailers sufficient compensation.

For the same reasons, the selected outlets will usually be small-scale operations. One retailer's activities will not normally encroach much on another's catchment area. All retailer-members of a selective distribution system can, therefore, and (in the interest of preserving what competition is left between them) must be allowed to serve, and even to appeal to, each other's potential customers.

The arrival of the internet makes such marketing efforts much more efficient. It allows sellers to address their advertising to specific customers, or to customers in specific areas, and to offer them the same goods as the local retailers at lower prices. Online sales thus have the potential to undermine selective distribution systems. Manufacturers will, therefore, seek to limit the internet marketing activities of the members of their selective distribution systems.

The *Pierre Fabre* judgment by the Court of Justice of the European Union ("the Court") is about such an attempt. For a proper understanding of the case it is necessary first to set out the legal framework for distribution agreements in EU competition law. The question will then be asked how *Pierre Fabre* relates to the earlier case *Copad v Dior,* which seems to point the opposite way.

2 The Legal Framework for Distribution Agreements in European Competition Law

2.1 Regulation (EU) No. 330/2010

The Block Exemption Regulation for distribution agreements[2] does not mention the internet. It does, however, define selective distribution systems:

> "Article 1 – *Definitions*. (1) For the purposes of this Regulation, the following definitions shall apply:
> [...]
> (e): 'selective distribution system' means a distribution system where the supplier undertakes to sell the contract goods or services, either directly or indirectly, only to distributors selected on the basis of specified criteria and where these distributors undertake not to sell such goods or services to unauthorised distributors within the territory reserved by the supplier to operate that system; [...]"

The Regulation exempts, in its Article 2(1), only vertical agreements that contravene Article 101(1) TFEU. It could exempt only these, as agreements not in breach of Article 101(1) do not need, and are not even capable of, an exemption. There was, hence, no need in Article 1 of the Regulation to differentiate between types of criteria for the establishment of selective distribution systems.

Outside the context of the Regulation, however, the Court and, following it, the Commission distinguish distribution systems that select members on purely qualitative criteria, and those that also use quantitative criteria for admission. According to the case law of the Court, the organisation of a network of selected distributors is not prohibited by Article 101(1) TFEU (and thus does not require exemption under the third paragraph of that article), if and to the extent that three conditions are met. Firstly, resellers must be chosen on the basis of objective criteria of a qualitative nature. These criteria must also be laid down uniformly for all potential resellers and not applied in a discriminatory fashion. Secondly, the characteristics of the product in question must necessitate such a network in order to preserve its quality and ensure its proper use. Thirdly, the criteria laid down must not go beyond what is necessary.[3]

The burdens imposed on the selected retailers may lead to a certain decrease in price competition between them ("intra-brand competition"), not least because it offers the possibility of excluding low-price distributors (whether they operate only online or both off- and online). The exclusivity created by the selection criteria will,

---

[2] Commission Regulation (EU) No 330/2010 of 20 April 2010 on the application of Article 101 (3) of the Treaty on the Functioning of the European Union to categories of vertical agreements and concerted practices, [2010] OJ L 102/1.

[3] Case C-439/09 *Pierre Fabre v Président de l'Autorité de la concurrence*, [2011] ECR I-09419, para. 41; Case T-19/92 *Leclerc v Commission* ("Yves Saint Laurent") [1996] ECR II-1851, para. 112; Commission, Guidelines on Vertical Restraints, [2010] OJ C 130/1, para. 175, all with further references.

however, distinguish the products from those of other producers ("inter-brand competition"), and thus enliven competition on parameters other than price.[4]

The Regulation also contains a provision that governs the prohibition of certain modes of sales that are relevant in the context of online marketing:

> "Article 4. *Restrictions that remove the benefit of the block exemption — hardcore restrictions.* The exemption provided for in Article 2 shall not apply to vertical agreements which, directly or indirectly, in isolation or in combination with other factors under the control of the parties, have as their object:
> [...]
> (c) the restriction of active or passive sales to end users by members of a selective distribution system operating at the retail level of trade, without prejudice to the possibility of prohibiting a member of the system from operating out of an unauthorised place of establishment; [...]"

We shall see below that the Commission considers the prohibition of internet sales by members of a selective distribution system a restriction of passive sales. As such, it usually falls foul of Article 4(c) of the Regulation.

The other point that can only be noted at this stage is that Article 4 requires agreements to have as their "object" said restriction. Much of the debate in *Pierre Fabre* was about how the rules of the selective distribution system in issue related to this requirement. What is more, while the articles of the predecessor to Regulation 330/2010, Reg. 2790/1999,[5] had no headings, Article 4 of the present regulation expressly mentions "hardcore" restrictions. From this arose the question of the relation between "restrictions by object" and "hardcore restrictions". In the recitals to the Regulation, the Commission refers to those restrictions that Article 4 labels "hardcore" as "severe restrictions".[6] In its Guidelines on Vertical Restraints ("Guidelines"), the Commission expressly categorises hardcore restrictions as restrictions of competition by object.[7]

---

[4] Cases 26/76 *Metro v Commission* ("Metro I") [1977] ECR 1875, para. 21; 107/82 *AEG Telefunken v Commission* [1983] ECR 3151, para. 42; 75/84 *Metro v Commission* ("Metro II") [1986] ECR 3021, para. 45.

[5] Commission Regulation (EC) No 2790/1999 of 22 December 1999 on the application of Article 81(3) of the Treaty to categories of vertical agreements and concerted practices, [1999] OJ L 336/21.

[6] Recital 8 and, in particular, Rec. 10: "severe restrictions of competition such as minimum and fixed resale-prices, as well as certain types of territorial protection".

[7] Guidelines (*supra* note 3), para. 23: "hardcore restrictions of competition, which are restrictions of competition by object", and similarly para. 96: "restrictions of competition by object and in particular hardcore restrictions of competition".

2.2 Internet Sales in the Commission's Guidelines on Vertical Restraints

By contrast with the Regulation, internet sales are the subject of extensive reflection in the Guidelines. The deepening of the analysis on this point over the previous (2000) version of the guidelines[8] is one of the main innovations of the present Guidelines.[9]

In the Guidelines, the Commission explains that the internet is a powerful tool to reach a greater number and variety of customers than by more traditional sales methods, so that certain restrictions on the use of the internet are dealt with as (re)sales restrictions. In principle, according to the Commission, every distributor must be allowed to use the internet to sell products. In general, where a distributor uses a website to sell products, the Commission considers that a form of passive selling, since it is a reasonable way to allow customers to reach the distributor. Even the offering of different language options on the website does not, of itself, change the passive character of such selling.[10]

Nevertheless, the Commission also acknowledges that a restriction on the use of the internet by distributors in an agreement is compatible with the Block Exemption Regulation to the extent that promotion on the internet or use of the internet would lead to active selling into, for instance, other distributors' exclusive territories or customer groups. In general, according to the Commission, efforts by a seller to be found specifically in a certain territory or by a certain customer group is active selling into that territory or to that customer group. As examples, the Commission mentions online advertisements specifically addressed to certain customers, territory-based banners on third-party websites, and paying a search engine or online advertisement provider to have advertisements displayed specifically to users in a particular territory.[11]

---

[8] [2000] OJ C 291/1; para. 51 is the only passage in which the Commission deals with the internet.

[9] *Brenning-Louko/Gurin/Peeperkorn/Viertiö*: Vertical agreements: new competition rules for the next decade, (2010) 2 Competition Law Newsletter 14, 18–19 (http://ec.europa.eu/competition/publications/cpn/2010_2_4.pdf).

[10] Guidelines (*supra* note 3), para. 52; this was already its position in the Guidelines of 2000 (*supra* note 8). This position is criticised as "over-inclusive and not reflective of the complexities of modern e-commerce" by *Velez*, Legislative Comment – Significant changes to the block exemption on vertical restraints, (2011) 32 ECLR 212, 216, who argues (at 217) that a distributor would not take on the cost of setting up its website in languages that are not spoken in its territory if it were not actively targeting customers outside its territory, so that language should be determinative in labelling an activity as passive or active selling. *Pischel*, Der Internetverbrieb nach der neuen Schirm-Guppenfreistellungsverordnung für den Vertikalvertrieb und deren Leitlinien, (2010) GRUR 972, 973, is concerned that "foreign"-language versions of websites blur the distinction between active and passive sales. His concern seems exaggerated: specific language versions might be seen as no more than the electronic equivalent to a notice to customers saying, "We speak English/Man spricht Deutsch" etc.

[11] Guidelines (*supra* note 3), para. 53.

We have seen above that there is a tension between the unlimited permissibility of sales over the internet and manufacturers' efforts to establish and to sustain systems of selective distribution. The Commission tries to alleviate this tension by allowing suppliers to require quality standards for the use of the internet site to resell its goods, just as the supplier may require quality standards for a shop or for selling by catalogue or for advertising and promotion in general.[12] On this premise, within a selective distribution system (as opposed to a system of exclusive distribution as just discussed) the dealers should be free, according to the Commission, to sell both actively and passively to all end users, including with the help of the internet. Therefore, the Commission considers any obligations which dissuade appointed dealers from using the internet to reach a greater number and variety of customers by imposing criteria for online sales which are not overall equivalent to the criteria imposed for the sales from the brick-and-mortar shop as a hardcore restriction.[13] Nevertheless, a manufacturer may demand that its selected distributors maintain a physical outlet with a minimum turnover; manufacturers may subsidise the additional expense of such outlets with a fixed fee; but they must not impose a cap on turnover generated online.[14]

On another point that was to arise in *Pierre Fabre,* the Commission in the Guidelines explains that under a system of selective distribution, those admitted as dealers may be prevented from operating their business from different premises or from opening a new outlet in a different location (where its compatibility with the selection criteria has not been checked by the supplier). The Commission does not, however, consider the use by a distributor of its own website to be the same thing as the opening of a new outlet in a different location.[15]

3 Case C-439/09 *Pierre Fabre Dermo-Cosmétique*

3.1 Facts of the Case

Pierre Fabre Dermo-Cosmétique (PFDC) was part of the Pierre Fabre group of companies. It manufactured cosmetics and personal care products, with a market

---

[12] Guidelines (*supra* note 3), para. 54.

[13] Guidelines (*supra* note 3), para. 56.

[14] Guidelines (*supra* note 3), paras 52(a), (c), 54. Concerning a cap on turnover generated via the internet, it can only be noted in passing here that the Bundesgerichtshof, Germany's highest court in matters of civil law, allowed a cap of 50 % imposed by a manufacturer of luxury perfumes on its selected distributors: BGH, judgment of 4 Nov. 2003, KZR 2/02 "Depotkosmetik im Internet", GRUR 2004, 351. For the time being, there is no immediate necessity to revise this jurisprudence: mere guidelines, such as the ones on vertical restraints, do not force national courts to fall in line in accordance with Articles 3(2) and 16 of Reg. 1/2003; on this point, see Case C-226/11 *Expedia v Autorité de la concurrence,* judgment of 13 Dec. 2012, not yet reported, paras 24–33. At any rate, the case before the Bundesgerichtshof concerned the abuse of a dominant position.

[15] Guidelines (*supra* note 3), para. 57.

share of 20 %. For these products it had established a system of selective distribution. As part of that system, sales had to be made exclusively in a physical space, that is, in a marked, specially allocated outlet. In this outlet, a qualified pharmacist had to be present.[16] The pharmacist's presence was meant to ensure that consumers could at any time be given all information concerning the correct use of the products. Consumers would also be recommended those products that were best suited to their specific health or care needs, in particular regarding skin, hair, and nails. Such recommendations were to be based on the direct observation of the customer's skin, hair, and scalp. As a consequence, all forms of selling via the internet were excluded.[17]

The French competition authority took exception to this. The prohibition of internet sales restricted the choice of consumers wishing to purchase online; it precluded sales to purchasers outside the "physical" catchment area of the authorised distributor. The prohibition therefore necessarily had the object of restricting competition. More specifically, the authority considered the prohibition of internet sales a ban on active and passive sales, contrary to Article 4(c) of Regulation 330/2010. According to the authority, the internet was not a place where goods were marketed, but an alternative means of selling which was used in the same way as direct selling in a shop or mail-order selling by distributors in a network with physical outlets. What was more, the products in question were not medicines, nor was a pharmacist legally authorised or in fact in a position to make a diagnosis, least of all regarding any adverse effects that the product might have on the user ("pharmacovigilance"). The authority also dismissed the argument that internet distribution did not lead to a reduction in prices.[18]

When the matter came before the Court of Appeal, Paris, that court referred to the Court of Justice the question whether an absolute ban on sales to end users via the internet amounted to "a 'hardcore' restriction of competition by object" for the purposes of Article 101(1) that was not covered by the Regulation but could be exempted under Article 101(3).

3.2 The Advocate General's Opinion

Advocate General Mazák noticed "a degree of confusion" with regard to the distinct concepts of a "restriction of competition by object" and a "hardcore restriction". Rehearsing the jurisprudence of the Court, the Advocate General emphasised that when it came to ascertaining the object of an agreement, regard must be had, inter alia, to the content of the provisions of the agreement, the objectives it seeks to

---

[16] We learn from Advocate General Mazák's opinion that in fact, pharmacies accounted for 80 % of Pierre Fabre's sales (para. 6 of the opinion).

[17] *Pierre Fabre* (*supra* note 3), paras 9–14.

[18] *Pierre Fabre* (*supra* note 3), paras 20–21, 24–26.

attain and the economic and legal context of which it forms a part. The anticompetitive object of an agreement may not therefore be established solely by using an abstract formula.[19] He also pointed out that the concept of a "hardcore restriction" was not derived from the Treaty nor indeed from Community legislation but was referred to in the Commission's Guidelines on Vertical Restraints. There was no legal presumption that an agreement containing such restrictions infringed Article 101(1). An individual examination was therefore required in order to assess whether an agreement had an anti-competitive object even where it contained a restriction falling within the scope of Article 4(c) of Regulation 330/2010, thereby rendering the restrictive clause ineligible for exemption under that regulation.[20]

The Advocate General also addressed the argument that internet sales by one retailer-member of a selective distribution system took unfair advantage of the marketing efforts that another such distributor made in its physical shop ("free-riding").[21] In the AG's opinion, given that the setting-up and operation of an internet site to a high standard undoubtedly entails costs, the very existence of free-riding by internet distributors on the investments of distributors operating out of a physical outlet could not be presumed. This was so particularly because a manufacturer could impose proportionate and non-discriminatory conditions on its selective distributors selling via the internet in order to counteract such free-riding. In this way, the manufacturer could ensure that its distribution network operated in a balanced and "equitable" manner. It therefore appeared to the AG that the general and absolute ban was inordinate and not commensurate with the risks in question.[22]

With regard, specifically, to the selection criteria applied by PFDC, the Advocate General found that the presence of a pharmacist at the point of sale enhanced the image of the products in question. In its judgment in *Copad*, the Court had held that the characteristics of goods are derived not only from their material qualities but also from the aura emanating from them. The Court had also stated that the characteristics and conditions of a selective distribution system could, in themselves, preserve the quality and ensure the proper use of goods, in that case luxury goods.[23]

In light of these considerations, the AG argued that it was conceivable that there may be circumstances where the sale of certain goods via the internet may undermine, inter alia, the image and thus the quality of those goods. This could justify a general and absolute ban on internet sales. Nevertheless, a manufacturer could in the AG's view impose appropriate, reasonable and non-discriminatory conditions concerning sales via the internet and thereby protect the image of its product.

---

[19] Opinion, paras 24–26.

[20] Opinion, paras 28, 30.

[21] This also works the other way round, i.e. some shoppers research products online but then buy them in a physical outlet. Some might even search online, and compare prices, while they are out shopping in the physical world. The question need not be pursued here.

[22] Opinion, para. 40.

[23] Opinion, para. 44.

A general and absolute ban on internet sales imposed by a manufacturer on a distributor was, therefore, proportionate only in very exceptional circumstances.[24]

Lastly, in the context of Article 4(c) of the Regulation, the Advocate General argued that the internet may not be considered as a (virtual) establishment but rather as a modern means of communication and marketing goods and services. A general and absolute ban on internet sales in a selective distribution agreement would thus forfeit the benefit of the exemption pursuant the Regulation.[25]

3.3 The Court's Judgment

The Court observed at the outset that neither Article 101 TFEU nor Regulation No 2790/1999 referred to the concept of "hardcore" restriction of competition. Instead, the Court directed its enquiry to the questions: whether the contractual clause at issue in the main proceedings amounted to a restriction of competition "by object" within the meaning of Article 101(1) TFEU; and whether, if the distribution contract breached that provision, it could benefit from block exemption under the Regulation or, failing this, it could be exempted under Article 101(3).[26]

The current Regulation, as we have seen above, does contain the phrase "hardcore restrictions". Nevertheless, the Court's steps of assessment can be read to say that "hardcore restrictions" is only a convenient label for all restrictions that are caught by Article 4 of the Regulation and whose presence in an agreement rules out their block exemption. Factually, there may be some likelihood that such clauses will also fail to pass muster under Article 101(3). The Regulation—any regulation—cannot, however, preclude the application of the Treaty. The latter is the higher-ranking law. With regard to Article 101, it is established that no agreement that is caught by the first paragraph is categorically excluded from exemption under the third, just as much as the fact that an agreement is of a type described in a block exemption regulation does not mean that the agreement is caught by Article 101 (1).[27] Regardless of the categorisation of a restriction as "hardcore" or otherwise, an assessment under Article 101(3) is a necessary last step in any competition law analysis. The Commission (now) shares this view.[28]

Turning to the prohibition of internet sales in PFDC's agreements with its selected distributors, the Court held that by excluding de facto a method of marketing products that does not require the physical movement of the customer, that contractual clause considerably reduced the ability of an authorised distributor

---

[24] Opinion, para. 54.

[25] Opinion, para. 61.

[26] *Pierre Fabre* (*supra* note 3), paras 32, 33.

[27] Case T-61/89 *Dansk Pelsdyravlerforening v Commission* [1992] ECR II-1931, para. 98.

[28] Guidelines (*supra* note 3), paras 47, 60.

to sell the contractual products to customers outside its contractual territory or area of activity. It was therefore liable to restrict competition in that sector.[29]

In keeping with previous judgments, according to which selective distribution agreements necessarily affect competition in the common market, the Court found that such agreements are to be considered, in the absence of objective justification, as "restrictions by object". By contrast, if and insofar as such agreements aimed at the attainment of a legitimate goal capable of improving competition in relation to factors other than price, they constituted an element of competition which was in conformity with Article 101(1) TFEU.[30]

The next question to address was, therefore, whether the prohibition of internet sales pursued a legitimate aim and did so in a proportionate manner. The Court emphasised that in the light of the freedoms of movement it had, in previous judgments, not accepted a ban on internet sales based on arguments relating to the need to provide individual advice to the customer and to ensure his protection against the incorrect use of products, in the context of non-prescription medicines and contact lenses.[31] Crucially, the aim of maintaining a prestigious image was also not a legitimate aim for restricting competition and could not, hence, justify a finding that a contractual clause pursuing such an aim does not fall within Article 101(1) TFEU.[32]

The last statement is surprising in its generality, but entirely welcome. The Court presumably means to say that further restrictions (those on internet sales) are excessive against a backdrop of competition that is already reduced between members of a selective distribution network (because of their compliance with the selection criteria): the prestigious image of the product is already ensured by these very criteria.

This statement is welcome because selective distribution based on the luxurious image of the goods distributed had in past judgments been accepted with few questions asked, not only with regard to perfumes and cosmetics, but also with regard to tableware and decorative items.[33] The idea of protecting the luxurious image of goods was embraced with outright enthusiasm in *Copad v Dior,* to be discussed below. It had also been established, however, that it was excessive to demand the presence of a qualified pharmacologist at the sale of cosmetics. Sensibly, the Court of First Instance (as the General Court then was) pointed out that conformity of those products with the applicable European and national norms afforded sufficient protection to consumers.[34]

---

[29] *Pierre Fabre* (*supra* note 3), para. 38.

[30] *Pierre Fabre* (*supra* note 3), paras 39, 40.

[31] *Pierre Fabre* (*supra* note 3), paras 43, 44 with references to *Deutscher Apothekerverband*, paras 106, 107 and 112, and *Ker-Optika*, para. 76.

[32] *Pierre Fabre* (*supra* note 3), para. 46.

[33] See, e.g., Commission Decision 85/616/EEC *Villeroy & Boch* [1985] OJ L 376/15, paras 24, 25.

[34] Case T-19/91 *Vichy v Commission* [1992] ECR II-415, paras 69–71.

Given that the restriction was in breach of Article 101(1), the Court next contemplated the prohibition of online sales under the block exemption Regulation. The ban on internet transactions fell foul of Article 4(c): according to the Court, such a contractual clause at the very least had as its object the restriction of passive sales to end users who wished to purchase online and who were located outside the physical trading area of the relevant member of the selective distribution system.[35]

In this context, the Court refused to read the phrase "place of establishment" in Article 4(c) broadly, so as to encompass the place from which internet sales services were provided. Undertakings in any case retained the possibility to justify their agreements individually under Article 101(3) TFEU. There was, hence, no need to give a broad interpretation to the provisions that bring agreements or practices within the block exemption, such as here the exception referring to unauthorised places of establishment.[36]

Equipped with this answer, the Cour d'Appel de Paris found the prohibition of internet sales in breach of Article 101(1) and further found that it could not benefit from an individual exemption under Article 101(3). The restriction was not indispensable because it was possible to organise adequate consumer advice with the help of a website, supplemented if need be by a hotline manned by trained pharmacists.[37]

4 Luxury Articles and the Free Movement of Goods: Case C-59/08 *Copad v Christian Dior*

The case of *Copad v Dior*[38] arose from a trade mark dispute in the French courts between, in essence, Copad and Christian Dior. Copad was a French chain of discount stores selling, inter alia, clothes. Dior was a French company that designed and marketed luxury goods such as clothes, cosmetics, accessories, and others. These goods bore the "Dior" trade mark owned by the company. Dior did not, itself, manufacture all the items marketed under its brand. Some goods were produced for Dior by third parties under licence. This was true, in particular, with regard to Dior lingerie, which was made by Société industriel lingerie (SIL). Manufacturing licensees like SIL may be, but usually were not, also part of the licensor's distribution chain. Instead, they supplied distributors designated by the licensor.

The licensing agreement between Dior and SIL allowed SIL to attach the "Dior" label to the lingerie it made to Dior's specifications. SIL was not allowed, however, to sell any of the contract goods to economic operators outside the selective

---

[35] *Pierre Fabre* (*supra* note 3), paras 53, 54.

[36] *Pierre Fabre* (*supra* note 3), paras 56–58.

[37] Cour d'Appel de Paris, judgment of 31 January 2013, case no. 2008/23812, p. 19. Thanks to Rechtsanwalt Mark E Orth for making the judgment available to me.

[38] Case C-59/08 *Copad SA v Christian Dior SA* [2009] ECR I-3421.

distribution system that Dior had set up. The licensing agreement between Dior and SIL specifically stipulated that "in order to maintain the repute and prestige of the trade mark the licensee agrees not to sell to ... discount stores ... without prior written agreement from the licensor".[39] As it happened, however, SIL's business hit hard times. The company sought permission from Dior to sell the lingerie to traders outside the selective distribution network, but Dior refused. When SIL sold to Copad regardless, Dior sued both companies.

When the matter ultimately came before the Cour de Cassation, France's highest court in civil matters, that court sought the ECJ's guidance on the interpretation of Article 8(2) of (now) Directive 2008/95 (Trade Marks Directive).[40] This provides that:

> "The proprietor of a trade mark may invoke the rights conferred by that trade mark against a licensee who contravenes any provision in his licensing contract with regard to:
> (a) its duration;
> (b) the form covered by the registration in which the trade mark may be used;
> (c) the scope of the goods or services for which the licence is granted;
> (d) the territory in which the trade mark may be affixed; or
> (e) the quality of the goods manufactured or of the services provided by the licensee."

The Cour de Cassation wondered whether this encompassed a licensee who contravened a provision in a licensing agreement prohibiting, on grounds of the trade mark's prestige, sales to discount stores. Secondly, the Cour de Cassation enquired whether in this situation the sale in contravention of the agreement was not covered by the licensor's consent required under Article 7(1). If the sale was so covered, the court thirdly asked whether the licensor could nevertheless oppose the marketing of the goods on the basis of Article 7(2).[41]

Advocate General Kokott argued that in respect of luxury and prestige goods, the reputation of the goods was generally relevant as regards their quality within the meaning of Article 8(2). Irrespective of the other characteristics of the goods, damage to the reputation of the trade mark could lead to the goods no longer being recognised, in the same way as before, as luxury or prestige goods. For those product groups, the Advocate General argued, a manner of distribution that damages the reputation of the goods may at the same time call into question their quality. Thus, if there were mass sales of goods bearing the Dior trade mark at reduced prices in a number of discount stores, with the attendant promotion, consumers could gain the impression that goods bearing the trade mark were no

---

[39] *Copad v Dior* (*supra* note 38), para. 8.

[40] Directive 2008/95/EC to approximate the laws of the Member States relating to trade marks (Codified version) [2008] OJ L 299/25.

[41] The Article reads: "Article 7–*Exhaustion of the rights conferred by a trade mark*. 1. The trade mark shall not entitle the proprietor to prohibit its use in relation to goods which have been put on the market in the Community under that trade mark by the proprietor or with his consent.

2. Paragraph 1 shall not apply where there exist legitimate reasons for the proprietor to oppose further commercialisation of the goods, especially where the condition of the goods is changed or impaired after they have been put on the market."

longer as exclusive as they used to be. It might be otherwise if such goods only occasionally appeared in discount stores. These were questions of fact, to be determined by the referring national court.[42] At any rate, a licensee acts without the licensor's consent in the sense of Article 7(1) if, by putting the goods on the market, he simultaneously commits a contravention within the meaning of Article 8 (2).[43]

The Court pointed out that the quality of luxury goods was not just the result of their material characteristics, but also of the allure and prestigious image which bestowed on them an aura of luxury.[44] Since luxury goods were high-class goods, the aura of luxury emanating from them was essential in that it enabled consumers to distinguish them from similar goods. Therefore, impairment of that aura was likely to affect the actual quality of those goods.[45] From this, it followed that no exhaustion occurred when the licensee marketed products made in breach of quality covenants in the licensing agreements, such as here SIL.

This reasoning is not entirely convincing. For a start, to say that the "quality of the goods manufactured by the licensee" really means their perception as luxury goods by the public is counter-intuitive. From the context of Article 8(2), it would appear that lit. (e) refers to tangible, physical properties of the goods themselves to which the trade mark is affixed, just as much as the other entries refer to tangible, objectively ascertainable circumstances of the goods' production and marketing. The Advocate General appears to have seen this without, however, saying so openly. Instead, she shifts the focus to the "damage to the reputation of the trade mark [which] could lead to the goods no longer being recognised, in the same way as before, as luxury or prestige goods".[46] The Court takes this even further when it says that "the aura of luxury emanating from [the goods] is essential in that it enables consumers to distinguish them from similar goods".[47]

According to the Court's own jurisprudence, however, to make this distinction possible is the essential function of the trade mark[48]; the trade mark is, so to speak, the sum total of the goods' reputation. The preservation of the mark's "aura" is specifically the task of Article 7(2). The trade mark has one or, according to the Court's recent jurisprudence, several functions, however widely defined[49]: it is, in

---

[42] Opinion in *Copad v Dior* (*supra* note 38), paras 31–33 and 35.

[43] Opinion in *Copad v Dior* (*supra* note 38), paras 46–47 and 50–52.

[44] Similar reasoning can already be found in Cases C-469/00 *Ravil v Bellon and Biraghi* [2003] ECR I-5053, and C-108/01 *Consorzio del Prosciutto di Parma et al. v Asda Stores and Hygrade Foods* [2003] ECR I-5121, with a critical discussion by *Enchelmaier*, (2004) 41 CML Rev. 825.

[45] *Copad v Dior* (*supra* note 38), paras 23–26 and 32.

[46] Opinion in *Copad v Dior* (*supra* note 38), para. 31.

[47] Opinion in *Copad v Dior* (*supra* note 38), para. 25.

[48] See, e.g. Case C-206/01 *Arsenal Football Club v Matthew Reed* [2002] ECR I-10273, paras 47–48.

[49] See, e.g., Case C-487/07 *L'Oréal SA, Lancôme perfums et beauté & Cie SNC, Laboratoire Garnier & Cie v Bellure NV, Malaika Investments Ltd, Starion International Ltd* [2009] ECR I-5185, para. 58: apart from the function as a guarantee of origin, the CJEU also recognises the

other words, a means to an end, namely to guarantee the origin of the product, to advertise, to portray the proprietor in a favourable way, etc. The trade mark is not an object of protection for its own sake. This is true at least with regard to the mark's "aura" as such: the mark does not *have* such an aura, it merely *transports* the product's aura; it represents and condenses the producer's efforts at image-building (through money spent on quality, advertising etc.) that have gone into the product. From the point of view of the consumer, one may doubt whether one distribution channel or another diminishes the value of the product as such.[50] Not surprisingly, the criteria for establishing a "quality" contravention under Article 8(2) are substantially identical with the test for a debasement of the trade mark under Article 7(2).

The difference, however, is that Article 7(2) presupposes that exhaustion has occurred under Article 7(1). Contraventions under Article 8(2), by contrast, prevent exhaustion from occurring in the first place. This is where the consequences of what might otherwise look like mere playing with words become worrying. If no exhaustion has occurred, parallel traders cannot distribute the goods safe in the knowledge that they will only be answerable under Article 7(2) if they deviate, to the detriment of the goods' reputation, from honest practices in their line of business. If Article 8(2) applies, the very source of the goods is poisoned. An honest trader will, as a consequence, not be able safely to handle the goods if the licensee has only supplied enough other discounters besides him. Whether such supplies have been sufficiently widespread will be difficult for the trader to find out, if not downright impossible. The licensee, for obvious reasons, is unlikely to be forthcoming with that information. Even if he were, the consequences under Article 8(2) are not a question of fact alone, but primarily one of legal judgment. This can only potentiate the uncertainty.

Licensors, on the other hand, can tighten control over their distribution systems by making distributors, whenever possible, licensees: for instance, the head distributors of "Dior" lingerie in each Member State would each be granted a licence of the trade mark for their respective territory, and then enter into as many sub-licences with SIL. This would require no more than the filling in of some standard form contracts; the production and distribution of the goods itself would continue as before. All this could be avoided if Article 8(2) were read literally, and Article 7 applied as hitherto. The solution in *Copad v Dior,* therefore, marks a problematic departure.

---

functions of communication, investment, advertising; for a critical discussion of this see *Enchelmaier*, The Smell of Success: L'Oréal v Bellure in the European Court of Justice and in the Court of Appeal, (2010) 12 European Current Law xi–xiv.

[50] *Velte*, Verbot des Vertriebs von Produkten über das Internet als Wettbewerbsbeschränkung, (2012) EuZW 19, 21, in the context of Art. 101(3).

5 Discussion

As we have seen, in *Pierre Fabre* the Court was adamant that the prestigious image of goods is not a legitimate aim for restricting competition, yet precisely this is the basis of *Copad v Dior*. There are some marked differences between the paradigms with which each judgment is dealing: in *Pierre Fabre*, the Court contemplated the very bottom of the distribution chain, in *Copad v Dior*, the very top. In *Pierre Fabre*, intellectual property rights did not play a role, whereas in *Copad v Dior*, a trade mark licence took centre stage. Similarly, in *Pierre Fabre* the question of the exhaustion of intellectual property rights did not arise which was, by contrast, at the heart of *Copad v Dior*. Finally, in *Pierre Fabre* the market-segregating effects of the agreement were of paramount concern to the Court, while that issue was not raised in *Copad v Dior*. Nevertheless, on close inspection the two cases raise similar questions. This is true, in particular, from the perspective of European competition law.

Ever since one of the very first judgments on competition law, *Consten and Grundig*,[51] it has been a fundamental tenet that the Treaty's provisions on competition and on free movement are complementary. The Commission recently confirmed this in the Guidelines:

> "Assessing vertical restraints is also important in the context of the wider objective of achieving an integrated internal market. Market integration enhances competition in the European Union. *Companies should not be allowed to re-establish private barriers between Member States where State barriers have been successfully abolished.*"[52]

The Court's jurisprudence on competition law, therefore, has repercussions on the law of free movement, and vice-versa. Intellectual property rights, moreover, far from being opposed to the principles underlying competition law, are instead an integral part of lively competition, and shape the conditions in which and the terms on which undertakings can compete.[53]

Seen in this light, it does not matter that *Pierre Fabre* looks at sales between retailers and end consumers (only such transactions are protected under Article 4(c) of Regulation 330/2010), while *Copad v Dior* is concerned with an earlier marketing step, namely, the delivery to a distributor by the manufacturer (which the licensee was in fact, even though the licensor lent the goods its name). It would not have made a difference to the outcome in *Copad v Dior* whether or not SIL had

---

[51] Joined Cases 56 and 58/64 *Établissements Consten S.à.R.L. and Grundig-Verkaufs-GmbH v Commission of the European Economic Community* [1966] ECR 429.

[52] Guidelines (*supra* note 3), para. 7; the italicised passage is a paraphrase of *Consten and Grundig* (*supra* note 51), 340.

[53] Case C-10/89 *SA CNL-SUCAL NV v Hag GF AG* ("Hag II") [1990] ECR I-3711, para. 13: "Trade mark rights are, it should be noted, an essential element in the system of undistorted competition which the Treaty seeks to establish and maintain"; *idem* in Case C-9/93 *IHT Internationale Heiztechnik GmbH and Uwe Danzinger v Ideal-Standard GmbH and Wabco Standard GmbH* [1994] ECR I-2789, para. 45.

delivered Dior lingerie to traders outside France: exhaustion of intellectual property rights is premised on the goods being put on the market anywhere in the Union, regardless of whether that market is in the Member State of manufacture or not. Similarly, it is irrelevant for the result in *Pierre Fabre* whether some of the selected PFDC retailers sold the goods, via the internet, in France or in another Member State. The consequence of the agreements in both cases was the same: goods could not circulate freely in the internal market, but were confined to particular channels of distribution. This is equally deleterious, no matter at which end of the chain of distribution the restriction is imposed.

It is also true that *Pierre Fabre* is not concerned with intellectual property rights, whereas *Copad v Dior* is. At a deeper level, however, the two cases converge: trade marks govern the branding of products and thus the easy recognition of goods by consumers, in competition with other goods that vie for buyers' attention. Selective distribution also governs a parameter of competition, *viz.,* certain pre- or after sales services, or the image of products. Both are, therefore, specific ways of shaping the conditions of competition on a given market; both allow those granting trade mark licences or selecting distributors to create a niche for their products in which they are to some extent shielded from competition, at least more than undistinguished goods or distributors. What is more, in the case of a trade mark licence for the production of goods, as Dior had granted to SIL, there is an obvious element of selection and quality control. For this reason, too, the two cases must not be considered in isolation. Instead, the policy considerations underlying each of them can be assessed side by side.

Likewise, the element of exhaustion or its absence does not amount to a decisive difference between the two cases. It is true that if no exhaustion had occurred the illegality of the initial marketing in breach of the licensing agreements would run with the goods all along the chain of distribution. Even if one were to follow the Court's judgment in *Copad v Dior* on this point, however, the practical outcome would be the same in both cases. This is because Article 4(c) of Regulation 330/2010 only allows sales to end users, not to parallel traders (which by definition are outside the selective distribution system). Any attempt to sell to such traders, be it by SIL or by a member of PFDC's selective distribution system, would therefore have been in breach of the respective agreement and hence prima facie illegal. The possibility cannot be dismissed out of hand that some parallel traders might try to use private individuals as "accumulators" in order to get their hands on sizeable quantities of the goods that are subject to selective distribution. This clumsy way of procuring supplies for parallel trade will, however, only ever be a fringe phenomenon.

Finally, an effect on trade between Member States is required both under Article 101 and Articles 34 and 36 TFEU. In *Pierre Fabre,* this aspect was more prominent because the internet is so obviously untrammelled by the borders between Member States, and thus an ideal vehicle for the integration of national markets that so far remain segregated. Yet market integration is also the backdrop to the Court's case law on the exhaustion of intellectual property rights: once exhaustion has occurred, the goods can be marketed by anyone anywhere in the internal market. In deciding when, where, at which price and in what quantities they market goods embodying their intellectual property, rightholders have to treat the entire internal market, in effect, as one market.[54]

Nonetheless, numerous examples can be found of the indefatigable attempts by pharmaceutical manufacturers at quelling parallel trade. Sometimes they invoke intellectual property rights, such as in the stream of repackaging cases,[55] and also in the "smell-alikes" case *L'Oréal v Bellure*.[56] Sometimes they rely on restrictions in vertical agreements, latterly with the—fanciful—justification that without such restrictions research and development would come to an end.[57] The targeting of the internet is only the latest phase in this regard and here, too, we see the two-pronged approach of deploying intellectual property rights (the ad-words cases) and restrictive vertical agreements (as in *Pierre Fabre*).

All in all, therefore, one can meaningfully confront *Pierre Fabre* and *Copad v Dior* with each other. As it turns out, the reasoning in *Pierre Fabre* is more convincing, if only because the consequences of the judgment in *Copad v Dior* are so singularly unappealing. Nevertheless, *Pierre Fabre* and the Commission's Guidelines point the way forward for manufacturers who want to salvage their selective distribution systems in the online environment. They merely need to ratchet up their requirements for retailers' websites. There appears to be ample wriggle-room for testing out what exactly is meant by "equivalent" criteria for websites and for brick-and-mortar shops.[58] If all else fails, the pharmaceuticals cases already offer a fall-back solution: simply reduce the quantities supplied to keen online sellers among the selected distributors to what the geographical catchment area of their physical shop is likely to be able to absorb, as measured by the

---

[54] Case 19/84 *Pharmon v Hoechst* [1985] ECR 2281, para. 23, and the opinion of Mancini AG at 2288, right col.

[55] See, e.g., Cases C-348/04 *Boehringer Ingelheim v Swingward* [2007] ECR I-3391, C-276/05 *Wellcome v Paranova* [2008] ECR I-10479; Joined Cases C-400/09 and C-207/10 *Orifarm and Paranova v Merck Sharp & Dohme*, [2011] ECR I-07063, with ever more intricate questions regarding colour schemes, fonts, font sizes and other minute details of packaging design.

[56] *Supra* note 49.

[57] Endorsed by the (then) Court of First Instance in Case T-168/01 *GlaxoSmithKline Services v Commission* [2006] ECR II-2969, paras 118–122, 273–274, reversed on appeal by the Court of Justice in Joined Cases C-501/06 P et al. *GlaxoSmithKline Services v Commission* [2009] ECR I-9291, paras 62–63, and with additional reasoning in Joined Cases C-468/06–C-478/06 *Sot. Lelos kai Sia EE* et al. *v GlaxoSmithKline* [2008] ECR I-7139, paras 53–57.

[58] *Seeliger* and *Klauß*, Auswirkungen der neuen Vertikal-GVO und Vertikal-Leitlinien auf den Internetvertrieb, (2010) GWR 233, *sub* 4d, are critical of the requirement of equivalence, and instead suggest that here, too, the question should be whether the criteria regarding the website are necessitated by the characteristics of the product. An even more radical stance is taken by *Velez*, Legislative comment – Recent developments in selective distribution, (2011) 32 ECLR 242, 246: "While it is still young, the internet is now a mature distribution channel that does not warrant special protection. Suppliers should be able to place similar restrictions on online sales rather than having to comply with confusing equivalency requirements in some cases but not in others."

sales achieved by the average of retailers in comparable locations, disregarding online sales.[59]

6 Conclusion

The Court's judgment in *Pierre Fabre* is a welcome re-assertion of the ideas of undistorted competition and of market integration against the contrary tendencies in *Copad v Dior* and other recent cases. We shall have to see, however, whether it will have any lasting impact. The Court's case law has more than once left unreconciled contradictory strands in the case law. This is often because the Court arrives at solutions ad hoc rather than based on systematic reasoning or with a design that integrates and harmonises principles and outcomes across a number of subject-matters. Free movement of goods, intellectual property, and competition would be ideal candidates for the application of such an approach, but the case law can be erratic and rhapsodic at times.

---

[59] See on the permissibility of this Joined Cases C-2/01 P and C-3/01 P *Bundesverband der Arzneimittel-Importeure and Commission of the European Communities v Bayer* ("Adalat") [2004] ECR I-23, paras 83–89, 102–103, 110, 123, 141; *Sot. Lelos v GlaxoSmithKline* (*supra* note 57), paras 68–73; on permissible controls by manufacturers as to which of their distributors have "leaked" goods to outsiders, see Case C-244/00 *van Doren & Q* [2003] ECR I-3051, paras 32–41.

Internet Competition and E-Books: Challenging the Competition Policy *Acquis*?

Simonetta Vezzoso

Abstract Relative ease of entry and rapid innovation are core characteristics of competition on the Internet, but, at the same time, a substantial number of successful Internet-based companies maintain very strong positions on their relative markets. A legitimate question, therefore, is to what extent the workings of "competition on the Internet" might differ from the more traditional market characteristics of the brick-and-mortar world, and whether competition policy as applied in this newer context would require taking account of special considerations. An interesting "case study" in this respect is the market for e-books, which lately has been the object of intensive scrutiny by competition authorities on both sides of the Atlantic. The brief discussion of the competition proceedings confirms that policy intervention in digital markets requires extra caution by authorities and courts, especially when there are network effects at work. More generally, casting Internet competition into the broader "vertical restrictions" picture can give rise to partly new insights for competition policy, such as, for instance, that being a "typical" discounter in the digital era does not preclude providing many of the pre-sale services customers value.

1 Introduction

The Internet is a powerful ecosystem with many, and increasing, uses, such as communication, commerce, data collection and processing, etc. From a service used by a few, it has rapidly evolved into a basic economic infrastructure,[1] as well

---

[1] Cf. *Lehr*, Measuring the Internet: The Data Challenge, OECD Digital Economy Papers, No. 194, OECD Publishing, 2012, at 11.

S. Vezzoso (✉)
Department of Economics and Management, Trento University, Trento, Italy
e-mail: simonetta.vezzoso@unitn.it

as into an additional market space.[2] Internet-related expansion is impressive,[3] and digital markets have so far experienced a steady flow of innovations, such as the introduction of mobile-based products and services, which, to some extent, have even disrupted web-based offerings.

Many of the core characteristics of competition on the Internet, like relative ease of entry, rapid innovation, price-taking behaviour, etc. would seem to suggest that the exercise of market power is rather unlikely. However, it is also quite apparent that many successful Internet-based companies maintain very strong positions on their relative markets.[4] One of the most relevant questions in this context is whether "competition law can be applied as usual in digital markets, or whether enforcers must take account of any special considerations when applying general competition rules in this area".[5] These "special considerations" might range from minor changes to our competition policy mind-set in order to adapt to the digital context, to shifting our focus away from specific products or services markets to more unusual competition dimensions such as for instance attention rivalry.[6]

An interesting "case study" in this respect is the market for electronic books, or e-books, which lately has been the object of intensive scrutiny by competition authorities on both sides of the Atlantic. Even if the economic impact of e-books on overall book sales is still somewhat limited, especially outside the US,[7] their emergence is deeply affecting long-established relationships within the book value chain, in particular between the content creator (the author) and the publisher on the one hand, and between the publisher and the retailer on the other. Moreover, as already experienced by other economic sectors, the so-called digital disruption engenders new dynamics between brick-and-mortar retailers and online offerings, both of analogue and digital content.

The paper proceeds as follows. Section 2 briefly summarises the main elements of the alleged conspiracy to raise e-books prices that involved Amazon, Apple, and five of the major publishers active in the US in the period around the launch of

---

[2] The trade and marketing of goods and services on the Internet via electronic commerce makes up the so-called digital economy; see OECD, The Digital Economy, Report of two Hearings, Competition Committee, 2013, DAF/COMP(2012)22.

[3] As noted by the European Commission in its decision approving Microsoft's acquisition of Skype, "the use of sites such as Facebook, Google+, LinkedIn and Twitter has more than doubled since January 2009"; see Case No. Comp/M.6281-Microsoft/Skype, 7/10/2011.

[4] See *Haucap/Heimeshoff*, Google, Facebook, Amazon, eBay: Is the Internet Driving Competition or Market Monopolization? DICE Discussion Paper, January 2013, at 2.

[5] Summary of the 19 October 2011 Hearing, in OECD, The Digital Economy, *supra* note 2, at 127.

[6] Cf. *Evans*, Attention Rivalry Among Online Platforms, University of Chicago Institute for Law & Economics Olin Research Paper No. 627 (2013), available at: http://ssrn.com/abstract=2195340 (accessed 19 November 2013).

[7] It should be remembered in this context that several countries impose higher tax rates on e-books than on paper books. Luxembourg and France recently decided to apply reduced VAT rates on the sale of e-books (3 % and 5.5 %, respectively), followed by the opening of two infringement proceedings under Art. 258 TFEU (Treaty on the Functioning of the European Union). A European compromise might be in sight, foreseeing a single rate for paper and electronic books alike.

Apple's iPad. Section 3 puts the alleged conspiracy into the broader picture of the forces and dynamics shaping the development of the e-book sector at that time, and in particular investigates the impact of the shift from the traditional wholesale to the so-called agency model as applied to the distribution of e-books. Section 4 reflects on some of the core principles guiding the competition policy assessment of vertical restraints affecting the distribution of books between the digital and the analogue worlds. Section 5 provides some conclusive remarks.

2 Apple, Amazon, and the Publishers: Competition Proceedings on Both Sides of the Atlantic

Physical books have been available for thousands of years,[8] also boldly withstanding the first waves of digital disruption. In fact, the growth in demand for e-books is a very recent phenomenon. The main technical characteristic of an e-book is that content is formatted digitally and made available to the public by displaying it on a computer screen or, increasingly, on a handheld device, such as a multi-purpose tablet,[9] a dedicated e-reader,[10] or a smartphone. Formats can be open, such as for instance EPUB and PDF, or proprietary.[11] Independent of the level of openness of the format chosen, publishers currently employ digital rights management (DRM) restrictions limiting uses such as copying, printing, and sharing (lending).[12]

In 2007, Amazon launched in the US a new and dedicated e-reading device, the Kindle, which largely mimicked the reading experience of a physical book[13] and triggered broad adoption of e-books among initially sceptical users.[14] The more

---

[8] The first known examples of writing date from the early 3rd millennium BC, and were on clay tablets. The craft of book binding itself possibly originated in India, binding together palm leaves.

[9] Tablets are portable devices providing a bundle of services, in particular, Internet browsing, e-mail, access to content, such as music and books, and to other entertainment offers.

[10] The first e-reading devices were released in 1998, but the switch to e-books in the general trade markets started only recently, with the launch of the Sony e-reader in 2006 and of the Amazon Kindle e-reader in 2007.

[11] For instance, Amazon's AZW formatted files can be opened and viewed with Amazon's Kindle e-book reader. Moreover, Kindle reading apps are available for PCs, tablets, and smartphones.

[12] Thus, for instance, Apple's Fairplay DRM is applied to e-books in the EPUB format and read on iOS devices, but publishers can decide to opt out of DRM.

[13] In particular, E-ink and E-paper technologies enable a "look and feel" display of texts similar to the physical print on paper.

[14] Outside the US, sales of e-books initially remained much lower. For instance, e-books revenues in France in 2008 still represented only 0.1 % of the total €5 billion revenues from book sales; see Autorité de la Concurrence, Avis no 09-A-56 du 18 décembre 2009 relatif à une demande d'avis du ministre de la culture et de la communication portant sur le livre numérique, at 6.

recent availability of further e-readers released by booksellers[15] and the successful launch of tablet devices with e-reading capabilities[16] are reinforcing the trend towards e-book expansion, also among younger readers. Six years on from Amazon's successful Kindle's launch, e-book purchases make up a rapidly increasing proportion of total book sales, especially in the US and in some European countries. However, and differently from the music sector, markets for book content are still to a large extent defined by language, and this could at least slow down the pace at which digital disruption might be affecting the industry.[17] Besides readers' natural and cultural disposition and preferences, the availability of digitized content is also decisive for the widespread adoption of e-books.[18]

Even if the economic impact of e-books on overall sales is still somewhat limited, especially outside the US, their emergence is deeply affecting long-established relationships between publishers and retailers. The results of the parallel US and EU investigations into alleged anticompetitive practices on the e-books market offer a comprehensive overview of the most significant changes taking place within the book publishing value chain.

Traditionally, at least in the US, publishers have sold books under the wholesale distribution model, pursuant to which publishers charge a wholesale price for each book sold to retailers, and the latter retain full discretion on the end price to set.[19] With the advent of e-commerce, publishers initially carried on employing the wholesale retail model when contracting with retailers, such as Amazon, which were selling physical books online, and did not see it necessary to amend the model even when Amazon released the Kindle e-reader in November 2007. Because of the different distribution costs associated with the online distribution of e-books as compared to physical books,[20] publishers offering e-books were able to set a slightly lower wholesale price than for physical books. After launching the Kindle, Amazon started a discount pricing strategy for e-books, charging consumers $9.99 or less for newly released e-books, a price significantly lower than the retail price

---

[15] In France, the Kobo e-reader launched in partnership with FNAC, for instance.

[16] The iPad and other tablets were first released during 2010.

[17] OECD, E-books: Developments and Policy Considerations, OECD Digital Economy Papers, No. 208, OECD Publishing, 2012, at 13 ff.

[18] In Japan, for instance, mostly owing to the limited offer of titles in digital bookstores, overall e-books adoption rates are the lowest in the developed world. Despite Sony's introduction of e-reading devices in Japan already in the early 1990s, the market for e-books has not taken up yet, see "Why Japanese readers don't like e-books", CNNMoney, 11 February 2013. Apparently, however, the markets for serialized mobile phone novellas and comic books, to be accessed via mobile applications, are booming, see OECD, E-books: Developments and Policy Considerations, *supra* note 17, at 18.

[19] More precisely, publishers usually set a list price, or suggested retail price, and then sold books for a wholesale price which was often a percentage of the list price.

[20] The distribution costs associated with the physical books are clearly higher because, for instance, physical books need to be stored in physical places, shipped, and returned books taken care of.

for hardcover books. In some instances, the price for e-books was even lower than the wholesale price for e-books charged by publishers.[21]

Obviously, publishers were much concerned by Amazon's marketing strategy. In particular, they feared that Amazon's low prices for new releases and New York Times Bestsellers in e-book form could negatively affect the sales of physical books, and especially hardcover titles (the so-called front list), which typically provided publishers with the highest margins per unit of sale. In the longer run, consumers' expectation about e-books' prices would have put downward pressure on prices for e-books and physical books alike, compromising publishers' margins and income. Moreover, publishers feared Amazon's growing power within the e-book distribution chain. Consequently, some publishers approached Amazon individually with the intent of convincing it to change its pricing policy, but they were unsuccessful. According to the allegations put forth by the US Department of Justice (DOJ)[22] and the European Commission,[23] what eventually followed was the agreement among five of the six largest international publishers of fiction and non-fiction ("trade") books active in the United States[24] to adopt a joint strategy involving Apple, with the object to raise prices for e-books.

In 2010, Apple was still new to the e-books market, but it was already a very powerful digital content distributor and a leading supplier of mobile devices. According to the DOJ and the European Commission, Apple intentionally and knowingly joined the conspiracy, as part of which the five publishers almost simultaneously signed vertical "agency" agreements with Apple.[25] Different but

---

[21] See US District Court, Southern District of New York, 12 Civ. 2826 (DLC), Opinion and Order, 10 July 2013, available at http://www.justice.gov/atr/cases/f299200/299275.pdf (accessed 19 November 2013), at 33.

[22] United States v. Apple Inc., et al., Civil Action n. 12-cv-2826 (DLC) (SDNY). The DOJ complaint was filed on 11 April 2012 and transferred to the same court already dealing with previously filed class actions. On the same day, the DOJ filed a consent decree indicating its intention to settle the DOJ action. On top of that, there was also State Action on behalf of consumers, eventually settled by the parties. Under the terms of the settlement, publishers must refund consumers who purchased e-books at conspiracy-inflated prices between 1 April 2010 and 23 May 2012, see Roberts, What the ebook settlement means for publishers, Apple and you, available at http://paidcontent.org/2012/08/31/explainer-what-the-ebook-settlement-means-for-publishers-apple-and-you/ (accessed 19 November 2013).

[23] Case COMP/C-2/39.847. In close cooperation with the DOJ, the European Commission opened formal proceedings to investigate practices on the e-books market in December 2011, after having carried out unannounced inspections on the premises of companies active in the e-book publishing sector in several member states in March of the same year.

[24] The publishing companies involved in this case are Hachette, HarperCollins Publishers, Simon & Schuster, Macmillan, and Penguin Group. Random House was the only one among the major publishers who declined to join the conspiracy.

[25] Apparently, the idea to adopt an agency model instead of a wholesale model originally came from Hachette and later HarperCollins, but met Apple's initial opposition, see US District Court, Southern District of New York, 12 Civ. 2826 (DLC), Opinion and Order, 10 July 2013, available at http://www.justice.gov/atr/cases/f299200/299275.pdf (accessed 19 November 2013), at 34. Eventually, Apple decided to embrace the same model it already was familiar with, being used to sell Apps through the App Store, id., at 38.

converging interests allegedly brought publishers and Apple to agree on a conspiracy to eliminate price competition in the retail market for e-books. On the one hand, by launching the iPad, Apple aimed to enter the fast growing e-books market with a profit and feared Amazon's power to set the market price at a very low level.[26] On the other hand, as seen above, publishers had at least three main reasons why they feared Amazon's marketing strategies in dealing with e-books.

The agency agreement provided that pricing decisions were handed over to the publisher (the "principal"), while Apple (the "agent") was to receive a 30 % commission on the price of every e-book sold through the iBookstore. Moreover, if e-books were sold through other distribution channels, their prices could not be lower than the prices for those titles in Apple's iBookstore. The so-called most-favoured-nation (MFN) clause, or across-platforms parity agreement, effectively protected Apple from price competition by Amazon and other online retailers.[27] Furthermore, prices for e-books were set according to a formula tied to the price of physical books, so that for most newly released general fiction and non-fiction titles e-book prices would have ranged between $12.99 and $14.99,[28] notably several dollars higher than the then-existing e-book price at Amazon, but lower than the hardcover price for the same book.[29] Whereas under the wholesale model a publisher received roughly 50 % of the hardcover list price from the retailer, under Apple's agency arrangement a publisher was to receive 70 % of the retail price. Thus, for instance if the wholesale price of an e-book was $13, as long as Amazon was selling it for $9.99, because of the MFN clause a publisher would receive only $7 from Apple.[30] In the long run, the agency arrangement could be in the publishers' interest only if the whole industry, and in particular Amazon, moved to higher e-book prices.

Upon the signature of the agency agreement with Apple, publishers' representatives met with Amazon separately to convince it to shift to the agency model for e-books, in order to set higher retail prices.[31] At first, however, publishers' attempts seemed unsuccessful. In the midst of harsh negotiations, publisher Macmillan even

---

[26] According to analyst reports discovered by Apple in June 2009, a price of $12.99 for e-books could have been a more profitable price point than Amazon's $9.99, *id.* at 28.

[27] Apparently, the MFN clause was first suggested by Apple's in-house counsel, and was previously used in one of Apple's wholesale music agreements, *id.* at 47–48.

[28] Apple insisted on the price caps "as protection against excessively high prices that could either alienate [its] customers or subject [it] to ridicule", *id.* at 65.

[29] *Id.* at 61.

[30] *Id.* at 54.

[31] Steve Jobs, Apple's CEO at that time, told his biographer Walter Isaacson that the publishers "went to Amazon and said, 'You're going to sign an agency contract or we're not going to give you the books'", *id.* at 84, note 47 and at 104.

threatened to "window" its Kindle versions of new releases,[32] to be sold 7 months after the hardcover release,[33] and Amazon retaliated by deciding to stop selling all Macmillan titles, both digital and physical. However, less than 2 days after delisting Macmillan books, Amazon gave in to the publisher's request to shift to the agency model.[34] Shortly thereafter, Amazon sent a letter to the Federal Trade Commission complaining about "the simultaneous nature of the demands for agency from the Publishers who had signed with Apple".[35] At any rate, by 2 June 2010, Amazon had completed agency agreements with the five publishers.

The shift to the agency model for e-books meant that the publishers participating in the conspiracy, which in April 2010 collectively accounted for roughly 50 % of the trade e-book market, gained the control of pricing for e-books. The immediate impact of the Apple agency agreement on e-book prices, and of the ensuing publishers' contracts with Amazon, was a substantial price increase for not only new releases but also backlist e-books, which were not governed by the agency agreements' price tier regimen.[36] In January 2011, Random House, which had kept out of the negotiations with Apple led by the other big five publishers, also decided to adopt the agency model, and immediately afterwards raised the price of its e-books.

Competition authorities in the US and the EU thoroughly investigated Apple and the publishers' conduct under Section 1 of the Sherman Act and Article 101 TFEU, respectively. In the US, while the five publishers all eventually settled with the DOJ, Apple proceeded to trial. Judge Denise Cote of the US District Court for the Southern District of New York confirmed in her Opinion and Order filed on 10 July 2013 that Apple had conspired with the publishers to raise the retail price of e-books. According to Judge Cote, Apple's role as a vertical player was to knowingly and actively participate in and facilitate the horizontal conspiracy to eliminate retail price competition and to raise e-book prices. Without Apple's facilitation and encouragement the price-fixing conspiracy would not have succeeded.[37] The District Court also made clear that "entirely lawful contracts may include an MFN, price caps, or pricing tiers", and that "it is not illegal for a company to adopt a form 'click-through' contract, negotiate with all suppliers at the same time, or share certain information

---

[32] As Steve Jobs noted in an e-mail sent to James Murdoch of News Corp, HarperCollins' parent company, holding back e-books from e-retailers can be seriously counter-productive for the publishers, however: "(W)ithout a way for customers to buy your ebooks, they will steal them. This will be the start of piracy and once started there will be no stopping it. Trust me, I've seen this happen with my own eyes", *id.* at 81.

[33] Under the Apple Agreement, seven months was the exact period in which new titles were under the obligations of price caps and MFN treatment.

[34] See "Amazon Gives In to Macmillan and Apple, and E-Book Prices Will Go Up", 31 January 2010, http://allthingsd.com/20100131/amazon-gives-in-to-macmillan-and-apple-and-e-book-prices-will-go-up/ (accessed 19 November 2013).

[35] Opinion and Order, *supra* note 25, at 90.

[36] As explained in the Order, "the Publisher Defendants did this in order to make up for some of the revenue lost from their sales of New Release e-books", *id.* at 96.

[37] *Id.* at 114.

with them". It is illegal, however, "for a company to use those business practices to effect an unreasonable restraint of trade".[38] When the agency agreements are considered in the context of the entire body of evidence "it becomes evident that the caps for the price tiers were the fiercely negotiated new retail prices for e-books and that the MFN was the term that effectively forced the Publisher Defendants to eliminate retail price competition and place all of their e-tailers on the agency model".[39]

Judge Cote set the terms of the injunctive relief to which the Justice Department and 33 US States were entitled on 5 September 2013,[40] while the trial to assess damages has been scheduled for May 2014. In line with but also adding to the obligations ensuing from the pre-trial settlements with the publishers,[41] the court's order requires Apple to amend its existing agreements with the five publishers participating in the conspiracy to allow retail price competition and to eliminate the MFN pricing clauses. Apple is also banned from entering into agreements with e-book publishers that are likely to increase the prices at which Apple's competitor retailers may sell that content. Additionally, Judge Cote decided to include the designation of a third-party monitor[42] to ensure Apple's full compliance with the court's judgement, possibly convinced by the Department of Justice's argument that Apple's existing internal compliance program was notoriously inadequate to the purpose.

3 E-Book Cases Across the Atlantic: A Platform Issue?

As seen in the preceding section, Amazon's struggle to keep the price control of the e-books sold via its Kindle platform was backed by competition authorities, which resolutely reacted to what they considered a hard-core conspiracy among Apple and five of the largest publishers to stifle retail price competition, and whose negative effects were immediately palpable, in the form of higher prices of e-books for consumers across the trade publishing sector. Following settlements with the publishers, the average price of e-book bestsellers according to some estimates fell from more than $11 to roughly $6.[43] However, taking account of some of the

---

[38] *Id.* at 132.

[39] *Id.* at 133.

[40] Case 1:12-cv-02826-DLC, available at http://www.justice.gov/atr/cases/f300500/300510.pdf (accessed 19 November 2013).

[41] The commitments offered by Apple and the publishers to the European Commission are also largely similar, see Summary of Commission Decision of 12 December 2012, Case COMP/39.847—E-BOOKS, [2013] OJ C 73/17.

[42] Salary and expenses of the external compliance monitor will be paid by Apple. He or she will work in team with the internal antitrust compliance officer, who is responsible for ensuring that Apple's senior executives across all of the company's businesses receive antitrust compliance training, and who will report directly to outside directors.

[43] See *Greenfeld*, Retailers Discount Big-Five Best-Sellers, Keeping Prices at All-Time Low, Digital Book World Daily (4 September 2013), available at http://www.digitalbookworld.com/2013/retailers-discount-big-five-best-sellers-keeping-prices-low/ (accessed 19 November 2013).

specific characteristics of competition in the market for electronic publishing, the allegations of anticompetitive conduct put forth by competition authorities, while remaining serious and credible, could be perceived under a slightly different light.

Network effects take a predominant role in the economic analysis of digital markets. Generally speaking, the presence of network effects creates incentives to herd with others.[44] *Direct* network effects arise where users of a specific good or service interact with each other, whereby the value to the users relates to the overall number of users of the same good or service, for example Skype users, whose utility is dependent on the overall size of the network. *Indirect* network effects arise where higher usage rates for one product or service increase the attractiveness of that network for another group, which in turn result in additional benefits for users belonging to the first group. Thus, for instance, developers create game applications for Facebook users attracted by the huge popularity of the social network, and Facebook users profit from the rich offerings of game applications to be played on that platform. Likewise, the more people with spare rooms use AirBnB, the more travellers are attracted to the platform, and the more users/travellers will list their own spare rooms.

Against the backdrop of network effects, a platform's main characteristic is to facilitate value-creating interactions between groups of users that need each other, but are somewhat incapable of establishing valuable interactions on their own, especially due to the ubiquity of transaction costs. More precisely, platforms should be regarded as complex arrangements aimed at solving the specific difficulties resulting inter alia from the presence of indirect network effects—or interdependent demand. Platforms are seen as managing users' groups (different sides of the platform) especially via pricing, such as, for instance, not charging anything to users creating indirect network effects (subsidy side), and charging instead the group of users attracted by the platform's popularity (money side).

As mentioned above, one of the most challenging questions pertaining to the workings of "competition on the Internet" is the extent to which competition dynamics might differ from the more traditional market characteristics of the brick-and-mortar world, and what this could possibly entail for practical competition policy.[45] The practices taking place on the e-book market in recent years, which have been thoroughly analysed by competition authorities on both sides of the Atlantic, might possibly reflect some of those peculiarities, as will be explained in the following.

---

[44] See *Rochet/Tirole*, Platform Competition in Two-Sided Markets, (2003) 1 Journal of the European Economic Association 990.

[45] It is already part of the accepted competition policy wisdom that the analysis of competitive dynamics involving multi-sided firms differs at least to some extent from that of single-sided firms, see *Evans/Schmalensee*, The Antitrust Analysis of Multi-Sided Platform Businesses, University of Chicago Institute for Law & Economics Olin Research Paper No. 623 (2013), available at: http://ssrn.com/abstract=2185373 (accessed 19 November 2013).

On the market for physical books, Amazon not only acts as a traditional reseller, buying goods from publishers and selling them to readers at a profit, but also as a "pure" platform when new and second-hand books are sold directly to customers by external bookstores and other intermediaries.[46] As seen in the previous section, until 2010 Amazon was, basically, a mere reseller of e-books. Interestingly, while distributing e-books via the wholesale model, there were also some platform-like indirect network effects. In fact, readers purchasing e-books via Amazon's Kindle store needed dedicated devices in order to be able to comfortably read them, and publishers' interest in participating in the e-book market through Amazon was likely to depend on the overall number of potential readers owning those devices.[47] At the same time, consumers were likely to purchase devices enabling them to read e-books sold via Amazon only if enough books were made available to them on that specific platform.

Against this background, Amazon was able, apparently, to affect the volume of transactions by charging more to publishers (indirectly, having them subsidize e-books sales via selling smaller quantities of physical books) and reducing the price paid by the other side, i.e. Kindle buyers. In other words, because of its control over the resale price of e-books, Amazon was able to promote the distribution of the dedicated e-reader, also at the immediate publishers' expenses. As noted above, Amazon at times was selling e-books at a price even lower than the wholesale price it paid to publishers. The effect, possibly, was that publishers were selling fewer paper books. At the same time, in indirectly subsidizing Kindle sales, publishers were helping e-books' expansion and Amazon's rapid platform development, and in the future publishers could possibly have profited from this expansion by selling more e-books. The much-publicized Amazon's decision to exclude Macmillan from its online platform, in the form of both e-books and physical books, is an unmistakable sign of Amazon's opposition to the adoption of the agency model. In fact, by keeping control of the retail prices, Amazon was able to promote the expansion of its Kindle platform. Allegedly, Amazon's sudden switch to the agency model in January 2010 was only due to the pressures deriving from the conspiracy described in the previous section of this paper.

What happened after the switch to the agency model is also very interesting. Put in control of the price of e-books, publishers stopped subsidizing Amazon's platform expansion through low e-book prices affecting the sale of physical books. Therefore, Amazon was forced to embrace strategies different from pushing the adoption of the dedicated Kindle e-reader in order to expand its e-book business. The decision to sell the multi-purpose tablet Kindle Fire, developing its own "ecology", and to promote the introduction of apps to read e-book purchased

---

[46] Another example of a pure platform is eBay, which does not buy goods from one category of users to sell them to the other category with a profit.

[47] See also *Manne*, Amazon vs. Macmillan: It's all about Control ("if not enough buyers own Kindles, there is little value (and some cost) to publishers in participating in the e-book market through Amazon"), 7 February 2010, available at http://truthonthemarket.com/2010/02/07/amazon-vs-macmillan-its-all-about-control/ (accessed 19 November 2013).

from the Kindle Store on a variety of different devices, can possibly be interpreted in this sense. Importantly, Amazon's move also had the effect of increasing interplatform competition. In fact, readers of e-books bought on Amazon's platform found apps that allowed them to read Kindle e-books on different devices. Thus, for instance, a reader using an Android tablet had the choice of buying e-books using the Kindle app or the Google Play feature.

At any rate, during the two years in which the agency model was in place, the e-books market went through substantial changes, and it is very difficult to predict what will happen in the coming years, or even months. Apparently, indirect network effects in the e-books market nowadays appear somewhat weaker than they were before the switch to the agency model. E-books purchased via the Kindle store can be read on a multitude of different handheld devices, such as an iPad, a smartphone, or an Android tablet. Therefore, publishers interested in selling their e-books via Amazon are not dependent on readers owning a type of dedicated Amazon device. Moreover, even if the specific Kindle e-reader is still very appealing, especially, perhaps, to generations of older or more traditional readers, it is increasingly popular to read e-books on multi-purpose devices such as tablets as well. In this respect, there would be value to consumers in buying a device enabling them inter alia to read e-books purchased via Amazon, even if not enough publishers were participating in Amazon's platform. Furthermore, some social (or cultural) peculiarities of the "product" book could be decisive in order to provide for some competitive dynamics of their own. For instance, social media versions of the more traditional book clubs could come to rival Amazon as platforms for promoting new books (front list, both hardcover and digital), even those self-published.[48] Finally, publishers themselves are increasingly aware of the importance of engaging with readers via social media in order to promote new books.

Right now, it seems unlikely that Amazon, despite its very high market share on the market for e-books, will resume what for a relatively long period did look like an irreversible march towards conquering a strong dominant position in the e-book market. The pre-trial settlements negotiated by the DOJ, the case the latter won against Apple, and the commitments accepted by the European Commission, are also likely to be influential in shaping the market for e-books on both sides of the Atlantic in the coming years.[49] It should however be noted that the commitments undergone by Apple and the publishers contain some relevant limitations as to the categories of books involved. Thus, for instance, textbooks and children's books are not covered by the settlement. It is also very likely that there will be forms of price discrimination outside the reach of the settlement.[50]

---

[48] The retail market for backlists is also likely to see the expansion of "new" players, such as Google Play, following the private settlement with the US publishers and other bilateral partnerships mentioned above.

[49] Resale price maintenance for print and e-books, however, remains the norm for several European countries.

[50] Cf. *Picker*, Book Prices are Going Up (Down) (or Both), 17 September 2012, http://www.mediainstitute.org/IPI/2012/091712.php (accessed 19 November 2013).

In light of some of the peculiarities of digital markets briefly mentioned above, publishers' fears back in 2008–2009 that Amazon's pricing strategy regarding e-books would cause them to sell fewer physical books as well, and that, eventually, they would end up being critically dependent on a powerful buyer, or gatekeeper, were not fully unfounded, it seems. While competition policy intervention in dynamic markets requires extra caution by authorities and courts,[51] it should also be stressed that book publishers simply waited too long before devising a *competitive* reaction to the threat first posed by Amazon's successful move into the e-books market. Possibly frozen in exaggerated piracy fears and/or having caught the music industry "syndrome" that led to the emergence among others of Napster, they failed to develop suitable conditions for a profitable e-book business themselves. Their belated, collective, "last resort" reaction was absolutely necessary in their eyes, and perhaps, even good for competition in the then nascent e-book market, but such a concerted move is hardly what competition policy is supposed to promote or even tolerate.

4 Vertical Restraints Between the Online and the Offline World

Unsurprisingly, the so-called digital disruption also engenders new dynamics between brick-and-mortar retailers and online offerings, of both analogue and digital content. As seen above with regard to the book-publishing sector, the most noticeable impact of the Internet on that specific industry has been the strengthening of price competition. Thus, in the case of Amazon's e-books platform for instance, its distribution costs are lower than for a traditional brick-and-mortar bookstore. Moreover, the price transparency provided by the Internet tends to put downward pressure on the prices of all types of retailers. For instance, even consumers who buy their items from "main street" stores often have certain price expectations based on online price checking prior to visiting the physical store for their actual purchase.

The benefits from competition among different distribution formats, or *intertype* competition, are not so easily acknowledged at the policy level, though. More often, intertype competition is considered with suspicion, and free-riding concerns overemphasized. As is well known, the current competition policy orthodoxy considers vertical agreements restricting intrabrand competition with benevolence based among other things on the reasoning that they could encourage retailers to

---

[51] Accordingly, Judge Denise Cote, when discussing the content of Apple's obligations following the finding of a conspiracy, stressed that she wanted the injunction to be tailored so that it would prevent collusion on price in the future and yet encourage innovation in a rapidly changing e-book business, see New York Times (9 August 2013), Judge Considers Limits on Apple's Future E-Book Deals, available at http://www.nytimes.com/2013/08/10/technology/judge-considers-limits-on-apples-future-e-book-deals.html (accessed 19 November 2013).

provide adequate point-of-sale services and prevent free riding.[52] Thus, it is considered that a whole range of vertical restraints, might encourage higher levels of promotional efforts across channels, by guaranteeing a minimum margin to retailers. Non-price promotional service efforts are offered by retailers to the user, so that the combined levels of promotion and service across channels is consistently higher than those that would otherwise occur in the absence of the vertical restrictions in question. Accordingly, producers might specify through agreement the particular promotion service that they want retailers selling their products to provide. In the well-known US Supreme Court *Leegin* ruling stating that all vertical restraints, price and non-price, should be evaluated under the rule of reason,[53] for instance, the case concerned a producer who was asking retailers to adhere to minimum stocking requirements, specific store merchandising arrangements, particular product display formats, specific procedures for product repairs and exchanges, certain standards for the in-store treatment of customers, etc.

Casting Internet competition into the broader "vertical restrictions" picture can give rise to partly new insights, for instance concerning the very occurrence of free-riding cases. Undoubtedly, the Internet has made product and service comparison easier for consumers through a substantial reduction of the transaction costs. Looking for a new lipstick, for instance, a buyer can visit a brick-and-mortar store, select the brand and the shade that she likes, aided by the friendly advices of the professionally trained shop personnel, and then back at home, or at the office, effortlessly search the Internet for the identical lipstick sold at a lower price by an online retailer. In the dissenting opinion written in the already mentioned *Leegin* case, Justice Breyer argued[54] that there had not been any significant change in circumstances in the past several decades that might have supported the majority's intention to overrule the *per se* rule against resale price maintenance as framed in *Dr. Miles*.[55] Possibly, the advent of online retailing, although largely ignored in that case,[56] could have stood for such a relevant "change in circumstances" likely to make the occurrence of free riding more plausible.

It follows that, possibly, an increasing number of manufacturers might want to use resale price maintenance today in order to control their brand image and protect their distribution networks, and the Internet was indeed the change that could have made resale price maintenance more palatable. Prior to the Internet, customers typically searched for products, and eventually bought them, during a trip to a limited number of stores, whereas time-consuming visits to multiple stores before making a purchase decision were reserved to more expensive items. Nowadays,

---

[52] See the EU Guidelines on Vertical Restraints, [2010] OJ C 130/1, para. 107 (a).

[53] *Leegin Creative Products, Inc. v. PSKS, Inc.* 551 U.S. 877 (2007).

[54] *Ibid.* at 919 ("I can find no change in circumstances in the past several decades that helps the majority's position"). See also Note: Leegin's Unexplored "Change in Circumstance": The Internet and Resale Price Maintenance, (2007–2008) 121 Harv. L. Rev. 1600.

[55] *Dr. Miles Medical Co. v. John D. Park & Sons Co.* 220 U.S. 373 (1911).

[56] See *Lao*, Resale Price Maintenance: The Internet Phenomenon and "Free Rider" Issues, (2010) 55 The Antitrust Bulletin 473, at 473 ff.

well into the Internet era, marketing studies show that consumers are increasingly engaging in "research shopping",[57] like visiting a travel agent for advice and then buying the holiday package online.

Critically, however, being a "typical" discounter in the digital era does not exclude providing many of the pre-sale services customers require.[58] With regard to the sale of books, for instance, a substantial part of the pre-sale services delivered by the traditional bookseller consists in explaining to the customers how compelling, or informative, the book is, and providing some further advice. The Amazon's Kindle platform does of course provide most of those pre-sale services, in part by organizing readers' reviews and recommendations, and providing "personalized" advice based on the individual customer's previous purchases and overall search behaviour on the online store, something that a brick-and-mortar bookstore normally cannot provide.[59]

Perhaps even more importantly, direct consumer knowledge could make at least part of the offline pre-sale services provided by retailers much less important. The consumer can find out most of the relevant information just searching the Internet, but this, it seems, still crucially depends on the complexity of the service or product at issue. The Kindle e-reader itself, however, could represent a very good example of the Internet having at least diminished the importance of knowledgeable retail staff in guiding the choice of novel or complex information-sensitive products. Originally, Amazon's dedicated e-reader was sold exclusively online, becoming quite popular without any live retail assistant or dealer demonstration. Amazon displays information on Kindle's full features and specifications on its website, and adds professional and customer product reviews. If early purchasers were possibly the more IT-savvy ones, later adopters have the additional benefit of previous users' reviews.

Furthermore, in the realm of Internet competition, it can be more difficult than in the analogue world to understand who is actually free-riding on whom. Consumers could browse books on the Amazon's Kindle platform, reading the associated book reviews on Amazon's user-friendly website, and then buy the desired book from a neighbourhood bookstore. Several mobile-web applications even aim at encouraging users to shop at brick-and-mortar stores based on their GPS location, such as FourSquare. Interestingly, and at least in the general trade category,[60] data would seem to indicate that e-books are not simply replacing print books, but that the former are stimulating demand for the latter.[61]

---

[57] Cf. *Hsiao/Yen/Li*, Exploring consumer value of multi - channel shopping: a perspective of means - end theory, (2012) 22 Internet Research 318, at 318 ff; *Gundlach/Cannon/Manning*, Free riding and resale price maintenance: Insights from marketing research and practice, (2010) 55 The Antitrust Bulletin 381, 393 ff.

[58] More generally, the wealth of information like customer reviews and professional product reviews etc. are bound to decrease the importance of the "prestigious" retailer as quality endorser.

[59] Contacts with real online people are very restricted, though, mostly limited to when the customer has a very precise and not otherwise covered service issue.

[60] Other categories would for instance comprise education, reference, professional, and children's books.

[61] OECD, E-books: Developments and Policy Considerations, *supra* note 17, at 5.

Moreover, online retailers are unlikely to worry if consumers browse at one store and buy from another. Actually, under certain circumstances, online retailers are even interested in incentivising activities by research shoppers, notably those gathering information on their websites and not purchasing any good or service from them. The marginal cost of the research shopper on Amazon's Kindle platform is close to zero, and it can actually create value for Amazon. In fact, the research shopper can still contribute reviews, and, most importantly, leave data behind, sometimes of a personal kind, which Amazon can mine for all sorts of purposes (even selling them, possibly).

One further point is that Internet-related technologies, and the amount of data they produce, could even make it somewhat easier to design contracts compensating offline retailers for specific pre-sale services directed to the customers in a specific geographical area, helping solve the intrinsic inefficiency of so-called promotional allowances.

Finally, several of the special retail services shaping effective intrabrand competition in the offline world are likely to be made of intangible services that simply cannot be free-ridden by online retailers, such as the shopping experience in engaging environments.[62] More generally, resale price maintenance, as well as other vertical restraints, can be particularly ineffective in inducing from online retailers the type of services that only brick-and-mortar retailers can provide. In this respect, the fact that the online retailer is selling at a lower price does not automatically mean that it is free-riding on the pre-sale services provided by more traditional retailers.

In sum, as the above-discussed example of vertical restraints aiming at solving the "free-rider problem" in the publishing market might have demonstrated, the advent of Internet competition would seem to require us to (at least partly) reconsider the current competition policy assessment of vertical restraints, although the overall general framework may not need to be called into question.[63]

5 Concluding Remarks

This review of e-books competition/antitrust proceedings on both sides of the Atlantic has identified several aspects that could enrich our discussion on competition on the Internet. The circumstances investigated involved complex, strategic moves by publishers and online retailers in the context of the fast-growing e-books market, and of abruptly changing relationships within the book-publishing value chain.

While the specific restraints undergone by the investigated parties in the e-books case, like for instance those involving MFN clauses, have been assessed exclusively in light of the alleged conspiracy, it is very likely that in the future platform-based

---

[62] Cf. "The future of shopping – Malleable malls", *The Economist*, 16 February 2013.
[63] See also OECD, Vertical Restraints for On-line Sales, 2013, DAF/COMP(2013)13, at 5.

restraints of a more vertical kind will be increasingly scrutinized by competition authorities[64] and courts. The economics of multi-sided platforms is already well underway to showing that there could be specific, additional reasons to deem vertical restraints procompetitive, but also to consider them anticompetitive under certain circumstances.[65]

Apart from pure platform-based issues, competition authorities and courts are already carefully scrutinizing relations between online and offline retailers. As the example of free-riding has shown, the full consideration of the implications of Internet competition might require some further accommodation to the new environment of the present framework guiding the competition policy assessment of vertical restraints.

---

[64] See, for instance, Office of Fair Trading, OFT welcomes Amazon's decision to end price parity policy, Press Release, 29 August 2013; Arbeitskreis Kartellrecht – Bundeskartellamt, Vertikale Beschränkungen in der Internetökonomie, Hintergrundpapier, 10 October 2013, at 20 ff.

[65] *Evans*, Economics of Vertical Restraints for Multi-Sided Platforms, University of Chicago Institute for Law & Economics Olin Research Paper No. 626 (2013), available at: http://ssrn.com/abstract=2195778 (accessed 19 November 2013).

A Note on Price-Parity Clauses in Platform Markets

Sebastian Wismer

Abstract Presenting recent cases and identifying potential economic effects of price-parity clauses, this note aims at evaluating certain business practices which have been employed by several internet platforms. Firstly, it provides a brief overview of developments in the *Amazon* case and the *HRS* case: both the Amazon Marketplace and the HRS platform compete with other sales channels and have imposed price-parity clauses, prohibiting their members from offering better sales conditions elsewhere. Secondly, this note summarizes economic insights on price-parity clauses, building on a particular game-theoretic model that matches certain characteristics of these "platform markets" and exposing further potential effects that have been (partly) identified by previous literature in related contexts.

1 Introduction

The Internet and related technologies offer convenient ways of accessing information and open up new trade opportunities.[1] In turn, e-commerce becomes more and more popular, and online sales already take a significant (and growing) share of retail sales.[2] This evolution imposes new challenges to all involved parties:

This note was written during the author's time as a research assistant at the University of Würzburg. The views expressed here are strictly those of the author and should not be attributed to the Bundeskartellamt.

[1] In 2011, more than 75 % of all German households had access to the Internet. 83 % of the respondents to a survey conducted in 2011 among German households that used the Internet claimed that they searched for information on products and services on the Internet; cf. Statistisches Jahrbuch 2012, p. 205.

[2] In 2012, online sales made up an average share of around 10 % of all retail sales in Europe, cf. e.g. http://www.retailresearch.org/onlineretailing.php (accessed 2 April 2013).

S. Wismer (✉)
Bundeskartellamt/University of Würzburg, Germany
e-mail: Sebastian.Wismer@alumni.uni-wuerzburg.de

intermediaries (e.g. operators of trade platforms) use new business models with specific terms and conditions, sellers discover new methods of distribution and consumers have access to an increasing variety of offers, while antitrust authorities may need to assess the effects these trends have on competition and efficiency. These tasks may be complex, as they necessitate not only applying established expertise, but also developing new theories to evaluate certain practices.

This note aims at fostering this evaluation process by presenting recent cases and identifying potential economic effects of a certain business practice employed by trade platforms and online travel agents—price-parity clauses. Firstly, it provides a brief overview of developments in the *Amazon* case and the *HRS* case: both the Amazon Marketplace and the HRS platform are heavily used by many consumers, compete with other sales channels, and, most importantly, impose price-parity clauses, prohibiting sellers/hotels that are active on these platforms from offering better sales conditions elsewhere. Secondly, this note summarizes economic insights on price-parity clauses, building on a particular game-theoretic model that matches certain characteristics of these "platform markets" and exposing further potential effects that have been (partly) identified by previous literature in related contexts.

2 Price-Parity Clauses Imposed by Amazon and HRS

Sellers are often active in several sales channels to reach a large number of potential customers. As sales channels typically differ in perceived costs and competitive pressure, sellers face incentives to price-discriminate across channels. However, if one channel is operated by an intermediary with some market power (being active in a certain channel may be essential for sellers to reach customers), the intermediary may restrict sellers' pricing decisions.[3]

2.1 Amazon Marketplace

The Amazon Marketplace allows third-party sellers to reach consumers over the Amazon websites. In return, sellers have to pay fees for each transaction that is conducted over one of the Amazon websites. In May 2010, the European

---

[3] Note that platforms like Amazon Marketplace or HRS employ the "agency model": sellers set prices and the platform charges certain fees or commissions. However, platforms may also use a mixture of the agency model and the merchant (or wholesale) model, competing with sellers (cf. e.g. *Muthers/Wismer*, Why do platforms charge proportional fees? Commitment and seller participation; SSRN Discussion Paper (2013), available at: http://ssrn.com/abstract=2204498 (accessed 2 April 2013)). The following discussion abstracts from these issues.

Marketplace platforms introduced a price-parity clause, asking sellers to comply with the following rule[4]:

> "[I]f you choose to sell on Amazon.co.uk, you need to ensure that the total price and corresponding item price of each product you offer on Amazon.co.uk are not higher than the lowest total price and corresponding item price at which you or your affiliates offer that product on any other non-physical sales channel."

Immediately after Amazon imposed this rule, many sellers complained about the implied pricing restriction. The Munich District Court issued an injunction, resulting in an exemption of used books in Germany.[5] Furthermore, a lawsuit was filed also by another German trade platform against Amazon (*Hood v. Amazon*, Cologne District Court).[6] Moreover, in February 2013, the Bundeskartellamt surveyed 2,400 marketplace sellers,[7] assessing Amazon's market position and potential effects caused by their tariff system.

2.2 HRS

In a similar way, HRS, the leading German online hotel reservation service, asked hotels not to offer better rates in any other (online) channel[8]:

> "HRS expects its partner hotels to offer it the lowest room rates available. The Hotel guarantees that the HRS price is at parity with or lower than the lowest rate available for the Hotel on other reservation and travel platforms on the Internet or on offer on the Hotel's own Web pages."

Other online hotel reservation platforms such as Booking.com and Expedia apply similar rules. In 2012, HRS attempted to extend this clause on prices to reservations made at hotels' reception desks and started warning non-complying hotels. The Bundeskartellamt started an investigation[9] and the Düsseldorf Higher Regional Court issued an injunction against HRS's warning letters.[10]

---

[4] http://www.amazon.co.uk/gp/help/customer/display.html?ie=UTF8&nodeId=200458310 (accessed 2 April 2013); Amazon has also applied a similar rule on its other (country-specific) European platforms.

[5] Cf. Munich District Court, file no. 37 O 7636/10, 3 May 2010.

[6] Cf. http://www.presseportal.de/pm/50038/2359407/amazon-wegen-preisvorgaben-von-mitbewerber-hood-de-verklagt-auch-das-bundeskartellamt-ermittelt-wg (accessed 2 April 2013).

[7] Cf. http://www.bundeskartellamt.de/SharedDocs/Meldung/EN/Pressemitteilungen/2013/20_02_2013_Amazon (accessed 24 April 2014).

[8] http://www.hrs.com/web3/showCmsPage.do;?client=en&pageId=standard-01869 (accessed 2 April 2013).

[9] Cf. http://www.bundeskartellamt.de/SharedDocs/Meldung/EN/Pressemitteilungen/2012/10_02_2012_HRS (accessed 24 April 2014). The Bundeskartellamt continued to view HRS's best price clause critically and was liaising closely with its foreign colleagues in this matter, cf. http://www.bundeskartellamt.de/SharedDocs/Meldung/EN/Pressemitteilungen/2013/25_07_2013_HRS (accessed 24 April 2014). At the end of 2013, the Bundeskartellamt found that HRS's best price clause violated competition law, cf. Bundeskartellamt, case B9-66/10, decision of 20 December 2013.

[10] Cf. Düsseldorf Higher Regional Court, file no. 33 O 16/12, 15 February 2012.

3 Towards an Economic Assessment

The cases just mentioned illustrate that several prominent platforms have indeed imposed price-parity clauses and that there is an ongoing debate about how to assess these practices. However, as the prevalent use of the "agency model" is a relatively new phenomenon in platform markets, the literature on platforms with endogenous seller pricing decisions and price-parity clauses in intermediated markets is relatively sparse.

Before discussing specific effects of price-parity clauses in platform markets, it seems useful to distinguish between different kinds of "price relationship agreements" (PRAs) under which sellers agree to guarantee that particular prices do not violate a certain relation.[11] Depending on whether the buyer who pays the price that is constrained by the PRA is directly involved in the agreement, one can differentiate between PRAs between parties and third-party PRAs. In the latter type of agreement, an upstream firm (platform or manufacturer) and a downstream firm (seller) agree upon the relationship between the seller's platform price and prices in other channels (in the case of a platform) or the prices of competing products charged to customers (in the case of a manufacturer). Usually the price set by the seller on the platform must not be higher than prices charged in other channels or for different products. In the case of PRAs between parties, a seller directly grants the buyer some guarantee that he will not offer the same product (1) at a lower price to other customers (across-customers PRAs or most-favored-customer clauses) or (2) at a higher price than competitors (across-sellers PRAs, also called low-price guarantees and meeting competition clauses).

While there are several economic studies on effects caused by PRAs between parties (both theoretical work and empirical evidence), the literature on third-party PRAs (in particular, on price-parity clauses in intermediated markets) is much less developed.[12]

In the remainder of this note, I proceed as follows: first, I summarize a study on most-favored-treatment clauses (conducted in a mobile application pricing framework) and studies on "no-discrimination rules" (imposed by payment card networks). Second, I briefly consult the literature on platform markets and trade platforms. Although this strand of literature seems to be closely related, it does not offer any further direct insights into effects caused by price-parity clauses. Third, I explain potential effects of price-parity clauses, mainly inspired by previous discussions of agreements between parties and related practices in vertical

---

[11] The following classification goes back to a report prepared by Laboratorio di economia, antitrust, regolamentazione (Lear) for the Office of Fair Trading. The Lear Competition Note "Price Relationship Agreements: Economic Analysis and Implications for Competition" (Nov. 2012, available at: http://www.learlab.com/pdf/lcn_pra_final_textefigures_1354270080.pdf) (accessed 2 April 2013) summarizes the initial report "Can 'Fair' Prices Be Unfair? A Review of Price Relationship Agreements".

[12] *Ibid.*, at p. 5.

structures. Finally, I present a model which illustrates that price-parity clauses can have both positive and negative effects on welfare if sellers face a certain channel-importance effect which is caused by consumers imperfectly searching for matching products: price-parity clauses affect the allocation of consumers on existing sales channels, even in the absence of pure foreclosure effects, collusion, or classical service arguments.

3.1 Literature on Third-Party Price Relationship Agreements

To the best of my knowledge, to date, there are only two sources that directly address effects of third-party PRAs: on the one hand, there is a single study on most-favored-treatment clauses in a mobile application pricing framework, and on the other hand, there are several studies on no-discrimination rules[13] imposed by payment card networks. However, both sources presume a specific industry structure which does not perfectly match all important characteristics of an e-commerce setup.[14]

In his study on mobile application pricing,[15] Gans assumes that application developers can reach consumers both via a platform and directly. He shows that a platform operator may be unable to charge "membership" fees to consumers up front. This is due to a hold-up problem which is implied by the seller's pricing decision (which takes place after consumers decided whether to sink the membership fee). Imposing a most-favored-treatment clause mitigates this problem, possibly allowing the platform operator to extract more rents by charging positive membership fees.

Within the literature on payment cards, there has been an ongoing debate about the interchange fee (i.e., the payment set by a payment card network which connects issuing and acquiring bank involved in a card transaction) for several decades. Interestingly, many studies are conducted under a no-discrimination rule, not allowing for sellers' price-discriminating between different means of payment. However, most of these studies do not assess the effects of a no-discrimination rule on profits and welfare. Nevertheless, Rochet and Tirole argue that lifting the no-discrimination rule would lead to an underuse of card payment services.[16] Hence, the welfare implications of lifting/imposing a no-discrimination rule are

---

[13] The payment card literature distinguishes between "no-discrimination rules" and "no-surcharge rules". However, in theoretical models, a binding no-surcharge rule usually has the same effect as a no-discrimination rule: preventing sellers from price discrimination. In the following, the term "no-discrimination rule" is used.

[14] With respect to price-parity clauses, the following analogy between the payment card framework and e-commerce may be drawn: different means of payment correspond to different sales channels, and a potential surcharge for card use would reflect price discrimination between channels.

[15] Cf. *Gans,* Mobile application pricing, (2012) 24 Information Economics and Policy 52.

[16] Cf. *Rochet/Tirole,* Cooperation among competitors: Some economics of payment card associations, (2002) 33 The RAND Journal of Economics 549.

ambiguous in their framework. While Rochet and Tirole assume duopolistic sellers but do not analyze the network's incentives to impose a no-discrimination rule, Wright analyzes monopolistic and perfectly competitive seller pricing in a similar framework, focusing on the network's decision on no-discrimination rules and the interchange fee.[17] He finds that under monopolistic seller pricing the card network prevents excessive surcharging by imposing a (desirable) no-discrimination rule and chooses the efficient level of the interchange fee. With perfectly competitive sellers, both the network and a social planer would be indifferent between imposing a no-discrimination rule and unrestricted seller pricing.

In contrast to the aforementioned studies, Schwartz and Vincent take each consumer's payment mode as exogenously given.[18] Allowing for elastic demand in a monopolistic framework, they find that the payment card network prefers to impose a no-discrimination rule. Welfare implications are ambiguous, mainly depending on the relative group sizes (exogenous ratio of card users to cash users).

Related empirical studies indicate that some sellers indeed price-discriminate by surcharging card transactions (if allowed).[19] However, a majority of consumers tries to avoid surcharges, taking into account price differences when choosing their payment mode.[20]

3.2 Literature on Multi-Sided Platforms

During the last decade, several authors have engaged in the analysis of multi-sided markets. Besides (distinct) user groups who can connect or transact with each other by using a platform, one typical feature of these markets is the presence (and importance) of network effects.[21] While platforms like Amazon or HRS evidently facilitate trade between two groups, it seems less clear to what extent network effects are important in such e-commerce scenarios. However, regardless of the

---

[17] Cf. *Wright,* Optimal card payment systems, (2003) 47 European Economic Review 587.

[18] Cf. *Schwartz/Vincent,* The no surcharge rule and card user rebates: Vertical control by a payment network, (2006) 5 Review of Network Economics 72.

[19] Interestingly, legislation on no-surcharge/no-discrimination rules considerably differs across countries. While imposing such rules is prohibited in the EU, member states may still generally prohibit surcharging card transactions (by law); cf. Payment Services Directive 2007/64/EC ([2007] OJ L 319/1), Art. 52(3). In the US, card networks are allowed to impose no-surcharge rules in most states.

[20] Cf. *Bolt/Jonker/van Renselaar,* Incentives at the counter: An empirical analysis of surcharging card payments and payment behavior in the Netherlands, (2010) 34 Journal of Banking & Finance 1738; *Jonker,* Card Acceptance and Surcharging: the Role of Costs and Competition, (2011) 10(2) Review of Network Economics, Article 4.

[21] For a discussion, cf. e.g. *Rysman,* The economics of two-sided markets, (2009) 23(3) Journal of Economic Perspectives 125; *Wright,* One-sided logic in two-sided markets, (2004) 3 Review of Network Economics 44, illustrates that "one-sided logic" typically does not apply in two-sided market settings.

answer to the latter question, one faces another difficulty: the majority of the literature on two-sided markets abstracts away decisions of group members that affect transaction values (apart from the basic decision whether to join a platform). In particular, sellers' pricing decisions (in case of a trade platform) are usually abstracted away. Although a few recent studies which focus on the effects of revenue-based platform fees endogenize sellers' pricing decisions,[22] these studies abstract from bypassing the platform and competition between platforms. Therefore, third-party PRAs have not been analyzed within this strand of literature.

3.3 Potential Effects of Price-Parity Clauses

As explained above, the literature on third-party PRAs (including price-parity clauses) is limited. However, in particular the literature on agreements between parties (i.e., agreements across customers or across sellers in non-intermediated markets) and on "classical" vertical structures[23] is further developed and identifies several potential market effects that may also arise in platform markets.[24]

3.3.1 Foreclosing Entry of Other Platforms

Imposing a price-parity clause prohibits sellers from charging lower prices on other platforms. Therefore, even if another platform (an entrant) sets low seller fees as part of an introductory strategy, sellers cannot set lower prices than on the established platform. Consequently, the entrant may not gain significant market shares simply by setting low transaction fees to sellers. If this was the only way to attract customers, price-parity clauses could clearly be used to foreclose entry.[25] However, although "price image" seems to be an important strategic device, platforms may find other ways which circumvent the price-parity clause of their competitors, e.g. offering additional services, or granting some forms of discounts to buyers that cannot be attributed to specific transactions.

---

[22] Cf. *Shy/Wang,* Why do payment card networks charge proportional fees? (2011) 101 American Economic Review 1575; *Wang/Wright,* Ad-valorem platform fees and efficient price discrimination, FRB Richmond Working Paper 12-08 (2012), and *Muthers/Wismer* (*supra* note 3).

[23] For a survey on vertical restraints, cf. *Rey/Vergé,* Economics of vertical restraints, in: Buccirossi: Handbook of antitrust economics, MIT Press, 2008.

[24] The following discussion is inspired by the Lear Competition Note and the respective initial report (*supra* note 11).

[25] However, in particular when talking about platform businesses where network effects may play an important role, it is not clear whether more competition results in higher welfare – a few large platforms may operate more efficiently (realize higher network effects and choose a more desirable fee structure) than a higher number of smaller platforms.

3.3.2 Softening Competition/Facilitating Collusion Between Platforms

Price-parity clauses may soften competition between platforms/sales channels: if sellers cannot price-discriminate, a unilateral reduction of transaction fees in one channel is supposed to reduce prices in all channels, not only in the channel in which fees are reduced (prices typically reflect average costs). Therefore, platforms cannot gain significant market shares by lowering fees and face weaker incentives to cut fees, resulting in a higher fee level.[26] Similarly, when committed on a price-parity clause, deviating from a collusive outcome becomes less attractive to platforms.

3.3.3 Facilitating Collusion Between Sellers

Price-parity clauses are supposed to result in less price variety across sales channels. This makes it easier for sellers to monitor price changes, possibly facilitating collusion between them. Furthermore, sellers facing multi-channel contacts may reinforce this effect (prices are linked across channels, i.e., both potential deviations and punishments should spread out across several channels).[27]

3.3.4 Signaling Unobservable Information

In many situations both consumers and sellers are only imperfectly informed about important platform characteristics (e.g. a platform's costs, price and service levels, reliability). In these cases, imposing a price-parity clause may also be interpreted as a signal to communicate such characteristics[28]: if a provider with a certain characteristic profits from a certain business practice while a provider with a different characteristic does not (and has no incentives to imitate the other provider "type"), observing the use of this business practice can reveal the provider's characteristic. In particular, imposing a price-parity clause may indicate that sellers rely on the

---

[26] The basic idea behind this effect goes back to *Hay*, Oligopoly, shared monopoly, and antitrust law, (1981–1982) 67 Cornell Law Review 439, and *Salop*, Practices that (credibly) facilitate oligopoly coordination, in: Stiglitz/Mathewson, New developments in the analysis of market structure, MIT Press, 1986, pp. 265–294. Both studies illustrate that most-favored-treatment clauses can sustain supra-competitive oligopoly prices.

[27] For an introduction to the theory of collusion, cf. e.g. Chapter 4 in *Motta*, Competition policy: theory and practice, Cambridge University Press, 2004.

[28] Note that HRS combines its price-parity clause (imposed on hotels' room rates) with a best price guarantee (offered to hotel guests who book through HRS). This practice seems reasonable, as it may signal a low-price image (makes customers aware that hotels are not allowed to offer better rates elsewhere) and it serves as a monitoring device (customers are more likely to report lower prices in other channels). For a related analysis of agreements between parties as signals of low prices, cf. *Moorthy/Winter*, Price-matching guarantees, (2006) 37 RAND Journal of Economics 449.

platform despite the pricing constraint, meaning that the platform must exhibit some distinctive features (e.g. low costs, good service, or many customers using it).

3.3.5 Reducing Search Costs/Lowering Search Incentives

If sellers comply with a price-parity clause, customers no longer need to search for lower prices (of the same sellers) in other channels. While the reduction in search costs seems to be desirable, lower search incentives may also support customer loyalty towards a platform, which, in turn, may also soften competition, and, possibly, may impede entry.[29]

3.3.6 Protecting Investments/Mitigating Free-Riding

If a platform needs to invest to offer certain (pre-sale) services which also benefit sales in other channels, a hold-up problem may arise due to free-riding: when offering (desirable) services, the platform faces higher costs (which should translate to higher fees). If sellers also use other channels which do not offer certain services themselves, the platform is likely to lose transactions when sellers can charge lower prices in these (cheaper) channels. Consequently, due to the external effect, desirable investments may become less profitable to the platform.[30] Imposing a price-parity clause mitigates the hold-up problem, as final prices cannot reflect all cost differences between channels, hampering free-riding.

3.3.7 Mitigating Double Marginalization and Other Price-Related Inefficiencies

Diverging incentives between firms on different market levels constitute a fundamental problem in many vertical structures.[31] In particular, sellers may face incentives to set prices which maximize neither channel (or industry) profits nor welfare. The double marginalization problem poses a prominent example: if a platform charges transaction fees, these fees increase sellers' costs. Under

---

[29] For an analysis of the interplay between agreements between parties and consumer search, cf. *Janssen/Parakhonyak*, Price matching guarantees and consumer search, (2013) 31 International Journal of Industrial Organization 1.

[30] This idea is directly related to the service argument presented by *Telser*, Why should manufacturers want fair trade? (1960) 3 Journal of Law and Economics 86. To a certain degree, price-parity clauses exhibit similarities with resale price maintenance (RPM). However, note that under RPM, a manufacturer fixes an *absolute* price level, while price-parity clauses only impose *pricing relativities*. For insights on RPM, cf. e.g. *Mathewson/Winter*, The law and economics of resale price maintenance, (1998) 13 Review of Industrial Organization 57.

[31] Again, cf. *Rey/Vergé* (*supra* note 23).

imperfect seller competition, final prices include another markup above these perceived costs, leading to prices above the level which would maximize joint channel profits.

Another price distortion which can arise in a multi-channel setup and may negatively affect the split-up of consumers on sales channels is illustrated by the model introduced below. Under certain circumstances, imposing a price-parity clause can mitigate such negative effects, as it is supposed to result in cross-subsidizations across channels, leading to lower prices in high-cost channels and higher prices in low-cost channels.

3.4 Insights with Competing Sales Channels and a Channel-Importance Effect

This section summarizes a game-theoretic analysis[32] which illustrates that price-parity clauses can have both positive and negative effects on welfare. Interestingly, the model excludes foreclosure effects and service arguments, illustrating that imposing a price-parity clause may be interpreted as a response to price distortions which are likely to arise in a multi-channel setup due to a specific channel-importance effect caused by a certain consumer behavior pattern.

The basic setup can be described as follows: competing sellers offer horizontally differentiated products and can sell their respective product both on a platform and directly to consumers. The two sales channels (platform and direct sales channel) differ in transaction costs. Furthermore, for each product, consumers' willingness to pay may differ across channels.

Consumers take a sequential buying decision: in the first step, they select their respective favorite product in one of the two sales channels, taking into account prices observed in the designated sales channel and their own preferences towards products. In the second step, they compare prices of their favorite product across channels in order to decide where to buy.[33] The initial distribution of consumers on the two sales channels (how many consumers select their favorite product in which channel?) turns out to be a decisive factor in the model, as it determines relative competitive pressure within each channel (compared to the other channel) and scales sellers' incentives (not) to specialize on one sales channel.[34]

---

[32] Cf. *Wismer,* Intermediated vs. direct sales and a no-discrimination rule; BGPE Discussion Paper No. 131 (2013), available at: http://ssrn.com/abstract=2212605 (accessed 2 April 2013). This section builds on the Discussion Paper.

[33] The motivation for this assumption is the following: in a multi-channel context, a "billboard effect" is likely to arise – being active in one channel may lead to additional sales in another channel. Furthermore, this assumption also is in line with the reasoning applied by the Düsseldorf Higher Regional Court in its injunction against the HRS price-parity clause (*supra* note 10).

[34] In particular, a refusal to sell in one channel leads to a discrete loss of all potential customers who select their favorite product in this channel (these consumers are assumed not to be aware of the seller's offer at all).

If the platform does not impose a price-parity clause, sellers' prices reflect transaction cost differences (which are determined by the overall platform fee level) and relative competitive pressure—if many consumers select their favorite products in a certain channel, prices in this channel are relatively low compared to the other channel. The difference between each seller's prices determines customers' channel choices. Due to double marginalization, an inefficiently low use of the platform channel is most likely.

In contrast, if the platform imposes a price-parity clause, it gains control over buyers' channel choices as sellers' prices reflect average costs (cross-subsidization between channels) and do not differ across channels. Platform fees turn out to be inefficiently high, resulting in an underuse of the platform channel (but high platform profits).

When deciding whether to impose a price-parity clause, the platform faces a trade-off between (1) having full control over consumers' channel choices (i.e., eliminating suboptimal effects of double marginalization and perceived competitive pressure on channel split-up) at the cost of a limited seller fee (due to a participation constraint) and (2) letting sellers have control over channel split-up (channel-based price discrimination) while not facing a strict participation constraint. The platform decides to restrict seller pricing if the initial distribution of consumers on channels is skewed (in order to mitigate price biases and extract rents), if its costs for processing a transaction are relatively high (in order to gain from cross-subsidization), and/or if seller competition is weak (rent extraction).

As the model assumes unit demand with full market coverage, welfare effects solely depend on the final allocation of buyers on sales channels. If the platform faces relatively low transaction costs, a price-parity clause is likely to result in a less severe underuse of the platform channel than unrestricted pricing, improving efficiency. In contrast, if cross-subsidization in order to compensate a cost disadvantage (the platform faces high transaction costs) is the main motive for imposing a price-parity clause, this clause is likely to be detrimental.

Within the given framework, a price-parity clause increases welfare by mitigating platform underuse if the initial mass of consumers who select their favorite product on the platform is smaller than the mass of platform customers in the first-best outcome. This is the case if the platform faces a relative advantage in transaction costs. However, if the platform significantly gains from imposing a price-parity rule, the level of final prices turns out to be higher than under unrestricted pricing, and consumer surplus is likely to shrink even though welfare may increase.

4 Concluding Remarks

Platforms that facilitate trade between sellers and potential customers often employ an agency model (letting sellers choose prices while collecting commissions). However, several platforms impose price-parity clauses, asking sellers not to offer better sales conditions (lower prices) in other sales channels. If sellers are indeed active in several sales channels and the platform charges significant fees, such clauses are likely to result in higher prices in other channels and lower prices on the platform (as long as sellers remain active on the platform). Although this logic exhibits similarities to the "traditional" discussion about (third-degree) price discrimination, there are important differences: (1) in a multi-channel setup, consumers are more flexible, as they may switch between sales channels, (2) the platform strategically decides whether sellers are allowed to price-discriminate, and (3) the platform's decision on imposing a price-parity clause usually has interdependencies with other strategic decisions (e.g. structure of platform fees).

Taking into account the characteristics of platform markets, this note illustrates that price-parity clauses can cause different positive and negative effects on productive, allocative, and dynamic efficiency. Unfortunately, the extent of all these effects seems difficult to assess in practice. Furthermore, to date, not only the theoretical literature that explicitly addresses the aforementioned effects is limited—there seems to be no empirical study that examines the effects of price-parity clauses in platform markets at all.

Platforms that successfully impose a binding price-parity clause need to have a certain degree of market power, and the prominent platforms mentioned earlier indeed possess considerable market shares. Therefore, there may be cases in which these clauses can be addressed both as (vertical) agreements between undertakings (which may restrict or distort competition) and abuses of dominant positions (as they may exploit sellers and/or buyers and may hinder competitors).

Price-parity clauses may reinforce the strong positions of the platforms that impose these restraints. However, as platform markets may exhibit features of two-sided markets, the "standard" reasoning may fail—the assessment of market power and price levels as well as the desirability of "more competition" should be scrutinized in more detail. Furthermore, beyond the limited insights gained from theoretical research so far, interdependencies with other business practices (e.g. combination of the agency model and merchant/wholesale model, platforms' offering complementary services, effects of certain platform tariff systems) also deserve further investigation.

Acknowledgment The author thanks Florian Bien, Johannes Muthers, Norbert Schulz, and participants of the conference "Competition on the Internet" for helpful comments.

FTC v. Google: The Enforcement of Antitrust Law in Online Markets

Ronny Hauck

Abstract In January 2013, the U.S. Federal Trade Commission (FTC) finally closed its investigation against Google based on Section 5 FTC Act. The inquiry was mainly related to "search bias" allegations and Google's "multihoming policy". This article will focus on the first subject. After investigating for more than 20 months and reviewing "over nine million pages of documents", the Commission's results can be described as disappointing. From an antitrust point of view, the FTC failed to answer the relevant questions for example with respect to the relevant product markets and the analysis of market power in online search. Following some remarks on the history, legal standards, and characteristics of Section 5 FTC Act and a discussion of the role of the FTC in U.S. antitrust policy, this article addresses these issues and proposes solutions not only with regard to the *Google* investigation, but also with regard to the enforcement of antitrust law in online markets in general.

1 Introduction

Like no other company, Google Search (hereafter "Google") has changed the use of the internet over the last 10 years. Also, no other company was as successful as Google in creating "web search" as a business model, including a "vertical integration strategy" in online services. The company's official corporate motto is "don't be evil".[1] Nevertheless, over the past few years Google has faced several

---
[1] See Google's Code of Conduct, available at: http://investor.google.com/corporate/code-of-conduct.html (accessed 12 September 2013).

R. Hauck (✉)
Lehrstuhl für Wirtschaftsrecht und Geistiges Eigentum, Technische Universität München, Munich, Germany
e-mail: ronny.hauck@tum.de

investigations by antitrust authorities in the United States and the EU and has paid more than US$500 million alone to settle investigations brought by the FTC.[2] These investigations concerned allegations of misleading advertising, but also the abuse of a dominant market position.[3]

In January 2013, the FTC closed an investigation against Google that had attracted a great deal of attention. The main allegation was that Google was manipulating its search results to favor its own (vertical) e-commerce services (so-called "search bias allegation"). E-commerce platforms like Kayak, Expedia, Yelp, and Amazon accused Google of misleading search users by listing its own services within the "organic" search results list (=horizontal, unpaid search results) in a significantly higher position than "vertical" services offered by its competitors.

This article will analyze the background and outcome of this investigation. In addition, some of the legal aspects important for the antitrust assessment of Google's business model will be addressed.

2 The Federal Trade Commission and Section 5 FTC Act

2.1 The Federal Trade Commission (FTC)

The FTC is an independent regulatory agency, established in 1914 by the FTC Act (15 U.S.C. §§ 41–58).[4] The Commission is headed by five commissioners, nominated by the President and confirmed by the U.S. Senate.[5] It administers inter alia the FTC Act, the Clayton Act, the Robinson-Patman Act, and the Lanham (Trademark) Act and has adjudicative, legislative, and prosecutorial functions.[6] The FTC proceeds either on its own initiative or pursuant to a private individual's complaint. Its Bureau of Competition and Bureau of Consumer Protection have jurisdiction for the enforcement of antitrust laws and consumer protection laws, respectively (supported by the FTC's Bureau of Economics). The FTC jurisdiction (regarding Section 5 FTC Act) is delineated by the "commerce" and "public interest" requirements as well as the requirements of "substantial consumer injury" and of "substantial harm" to the competitive process.[7]

---

[2] See e.g. the U.S. Department of Justice's press release on 24 August 2011, available at: http://www.justice.gov/opa/pr/2011/August/11-dag-1078.html (accessed 12 September 2013).

[3] For the European Commission's Antitrust investigation against Google since 2010 (case COMP/C-3/39.740) see http://europa.eu/rapid/press-release_IP-10-1624_en.htm?locale=en (accessed 12 September 2013).

[4] See in detail *Winerman*, The Origins of the FTC: Concentration, Cooperation, Control and Competition, (2003–2004) 71 Antitrust L.J. 1.

[5] 15 U.S.C. §§ 41.

[6] American Bar Association, FTC Practice and Procedure Manual (2007), chapter I, at 2 ff.

[7] American Bar Association, *supra* note 6, chapter I, at 4.

2.2 Section 5 FTC Act

The FTC launched the investigation against Google based on Section 5 FTC Act (15 U.S.C. § 45).[8] Under Section 5(a) "unfair methods of competition ... and unfair or deceptive acts or practices are ... declared unlawful". Compared to German law, Section 5 is located at the interface between unfair competition law (*Lauterkeitsrecht*), consumer protection law, and antitrust law. Based on Section 5, the FTC has a broad mandate to enforce antitrust and consumer protection law.[9] In contrast, the FTC cannot directly enforce Sections 1 and 2 of the Sherman Act.[10]

The focus of Section 5 is on preventing and remedying harm to the competitive process and consumer harm. Section 5 was designed to fill "statutory gaps" in the Sherman and Clayton Acts.[11] Thus, Section 5 FTC Act has a broad scope, in particular "broader than the Sherman Act".[12] It covers violations of the other antitrust laws (regardless of presence of specific intent) including conduct violating even only the spirit of these laws ("spirit theory"[13]), conduct violating recognized standards of fair business behavior, conduct violating competition policy as framed by the FTC, and (other) unfair or deceptive acts and practices. The details of the scope of Section 5 have been determined by the courts.

In case of breaches of Section 5 FTC Act, the FTC is empowered to take all remedies necessary to eliminate the unfair or deceptive trade practices. These remedies are prospective and preventive rather than compensatory, punitive or structural. In general, the FTC issues cease and desist orders. The FTC can bring actions for civil penalties in federal district court for violations of such orders, but no treble damages actions. An investigation may also be terminated by settlement.[14] If the FTC concludes that a violation of Section 5 has occurred, it issues a statement of objections ("complaint") pursuant to specific statutes (e.g. Section 5(b) FTC Act or Section 4 Administrative Procedure Act). The respondent is entitled to a hearing before an order is issued and has 14 days from service of the complaint to file an answer. FTC's final decisions may be appealed to the relevant U.S. Court of Appeals.

---

[8] Leading cases based on Section 5 FTC Act are *FTC v. Cement Inst.*, 333 U.S. 683 (1948); *Grand Union Co. v. FTC*, 300 F.2d 92 (2d Cir. 1962); *FTC v. Brown Shoe Co.*, 384 U.S. 316 (1966); *FTC v. Sperry & Hutchinson*, 405 U.S. 233 (1972).

[9] *Corgill*, in Henning-Bodewig (ed.), International Handbook on Unfair Competition, 2013, para. 26 No 33 ff.

[10] See in detail *Hovenkamp*, The Federal Trade Commission and the Sherman Act, (2010) 62 Fla. L. Rev. 871; American Bar Association, *supra* note 6, chapter II, at 12 ff.

[11] *Kovacic/Winerman*, Competition Policy and the Application of Section 5 of the Federal Trade Commission Act, (2009–2010) 76 Antitrust L.J. 929, at 935.

[12] *FTC v. Brown Shoe Co.*, 384 U.S. 316 (1966).

[13] See *FTC v. Brown Shoe Co.*, 384 U.S. 316 (1966).

[14] However, some authors call such settlement agreements "weak substitutes for decisions by the appellate courts that affirm FTC rulings", *Kovacic/Winerman*, *supra* note 11, at 941.

In theory, Section 5 had the potential to make the FTC the preeminent vehicle for setting competition policy in the United States.[15] Nevertheless, since the mid-1970s, courts have been highly skeptical of the FTC's expanded application of Section 5 beyond established boundaries of other antitrust statutes. In consequence, Section 5 FTC Act has played a comparatively insignificant role in recent U.S. antitrust policy.[16] This is unlikely to be changed by the—highly anticipated but ultimately disappointing—outcome of the *Google* investigation (see *infra* at Sect. 2.3.2).

2.3 The Google *Investigation*

2.3.1 Allegations

The FTC accused Google of violating Section 5 FTC Act through several acts. First of all, Google was accused of manipulating its search results as mentioned above ("search bias allegation"). The Commission was concerned that Google might display links to its own vertical search services above the links to other, non-Google content found by its search engine. Another allegation concerned Google's "multihoming policy". In its standard commercial license terms for "AdWords", the search engine's advertising marketplace, the contracting parties were prohibited by Google from using competing online services. Finally, Google was accused of extracting information (including copyrighted content) from other websites during the search and display of results ("scraping").[17] This article will focus on the search bias allegation.

2.3.2 Chronology and Outcome

In June 2011 the FTC formally announced that it was investigating Google based on Section 5 FTC Act relating to inter alia the search bias allegation. In the course of the investigation, Google's Chairman *Eric Schmidt* testified before the United States Senate Judiciary Committee/Subcommittee on Antitrust on 21 September 2012. On 3 January 2013, the FTC closed its investigation by a 5-0 decision: "In sum, we find that the evidence presented ... does not support the allegation[s]".[18]

---

[15] *Kovacic/Winerman, supra* note 11, at 932.

[16] *Kovacic/Winerman, supra* note 11, at 933–935.

[17] Statement of the Federal Trade Commission Regarding Google's Search Practices: In the Matter of Google Inc., FTC File Number 111-0163, 3 January 2013, available at: http://www.ftc.gov/public-statements/2013/01/statement-federal-trade-commission-regarding-googles-search-practices (accessed 12 September 2013); Statement of Commissioner Maureen K. Ohlhausen, In the Matter of Google Inc. FTC File Number 111-0163, 3 January 2013, available at: http://www.ftc.gov/os/2013/01/130103 googlesearchohlhausenstmt.pdf (accessed 12 September 2013).

[18] Statement of the Federal Trade Commission, *supra* note 17.

In its final statement, the FTC concludes (related to the search bias allegation) that Google adopted the design changes and the changes of the search algorithms only to improve the quality of its (general and specialized) search results. Any negative impact on actual or potential competitors was incidental since adverse effects on competitors are a common byproduct of "competition on the merits" and the competitive process that the law encourages. The FTC found that Google's conduct may harm competitors, but does not harm competition and consumers.[19] Nonetheless, Google announced its intention to enter into "voluntary commitments" with the FTC. First of all, Google will provide a mechanism that allows websites to opt out of being displayed in specialized (vertical) search results but remain in the organic search results. Secondly, Google confirmed that particular restrictions in the General Terms and Conditions of the AdWords search advertising platform will be eliminated.[20]

This outcome has been heavily criticized.[21] FTC Commissioner *Rosch* found that "after promising an elephant more than a year ago, the Commission instead has brought forth a couple of mice".[22] Google's commitments are considered barely enforceable.[23] After all, the FTC inquiry against Google raises more questions than answers. In particular, important questions regarding the enforcement of antitrust law in online markets were not answered.

3 The *Google* Investigation: A Different Perspective

The antitrust assessment of online services and, in particular, of search engines is certainly a challenging task. The following remarks will highlight some significant points in applying Section 5 FTC Act and, in general, the other antitrust laws with regard to the FTC's search bias allegation against Google.

---

[19] Statement of the Federal Trade Commission, *supra* note 17. However, in his statement Commissioner *Rosch* expressed "strong concerns" about the alleged scraping and Google's multihoming restrictions, Concurring and Dissenting Statement of Commissioner J. Thomas Rosch Regarding Google's Search Practices: In the Matter of Google Inc., FTC File No. 111-0163, 3 January 2013, available at: http://www.ftc.gov/speeches/rosch/130103googlesearchstmt.pdf (accessed 12 September 2013).

[20] Google's "Letter of Commitment" to FTC Chairman *Leibowitz* is available at http://www.ftc.gov/os/2013/01/130103googleletterchairmanleibowitz.pdf (accessed 12 September 2013).

[21] See e.g. former FTC Commissioner and Chairman *William Kovacic* on bloomberg.com: "The agency set high expectations and gave signals they were going to do something bold. They painted themselves into a corner", available at: http://www.bloomberg.com/news/2012-12-17/google-said-to-end-ftc-probe-with-letter-promising-change.html (accessed 12 September 2013).

[22] Concurring and Dissenting Statement of Commissioner J. Thomas Rosch, *supra* note 19.

[23] "Close to worthless" (former FTC Commissioner and Chairman *William Kovacic*), available at: http://www.bloomberg.com/news/2012-12-17/google-said-to-end-ftc-probe-with-letter-promising-change.html (accessed 12 September 2013).

3.1 Search Engines and Section 5 FTC Act

To constitute a violation of Section 5 FTC Act, Google's behavior (notably the search bias allegation) would need to be an "unfair method of competition". This is invariably the case if Google's behavior violated the other antitrust laws, such as Section 2 Sherman Act (exclusionary conduct/monopolization).[24] Otherwise, the FTC has to prove that Google's behavior violates Section 5 in a different way.

3.2 Search Engines and Antitrust Law

Section 2 Sherman Act requires the FTC to define the relevant product market(s). In an investigation under Section 5 FTC Act, the FTC has to additionally prove that Google harms consumers. That leads directly to the question *which* consumer is actually affected by Google's behavior. Broadly speaking, two types of products exist in the search engine business: "general search" and "specialized/product search". If these products belong to different product markets, Google could have violated the antitrust laws if it has market power in "general search" and abuses this dominant position to hinder actual rivals and/or to foreclose the market entry of potential competitors on the "specialized search" market.

3.3 The Relevant Product Market

The definition of the relevant product market under Section 5 FTC Act follows the same principles as those under the Sherman Act and the Clayton Act. The standard tool is the hypothetical monopoly test. The relevant product market includes all products to which consumers would most likely switch in response to a relative price rise by a "small but significant and nontransitory" amount (so-called "SSNIP-test").[25]

For the issue of interchangeability the wishes and preferences of the opposite side of the market are essential (demand-side substitution). Regarding search engines, the search users as well as the companies who wish to place advertisements on the result pages (advertisers) are relevant. Thus, these markets can be

---

[24] For specific problems regarding the application of Section 2 Sherman Act on Google's business practices see *Manne/Wright*, Google and the Limits of Antitrust: the Case Against the Case Against Google, (2011) 34 Harvard Journal of Law & Public Policy 171.

[25] In the EU, the relevant product market comprises all those products and/or services which are regarded as interchangeable or substitutable by the consumer by reason of the products' characteristics, their prices and their intended use; see Commission Notice on the definition of relevant market for the purposes of Community competition law, [1997] OJ C 372/5; *Averitt/Lande* endorse the alternative "consumer choice model", in *Averitt/Lande*, Using the "Consumer Choice" Approach to Antitrust Law, (2007) 74 Antitrust L.J. 175.

characterized as "multi-sided" or "two-sided" markets. To such markets, the common tools for the definition of product markets can be applied only in a modified way.[26]

3.3.1 Market Definition

From the search user's perspective, it is rather unlikely that one would switch from specialized/product search to general search while searching for specific products. Thus, the products "general search" and "specialized search" are not interchangeable. On the other hand, the search user would likely switch to other specialized search engines and e-commerce platforms like Kayak and Expedia. Therefore, these products can be interchanged with Google's specialized search. In the category "general search", however, Google's product could be replaced by the service offered by general search providers like Bing and Yahoo!, but not by the above-mentioned e-commerce platforms.

Thus, some consider "general search" and "specialized search" as different products and markets. Since Google has market power on the "general search" market,[27] it cannot be ruled out that Google may try to leverage its market power to the downstream market (specialized search). According to another opinion, the mentioned products belong to one product market; leveraging of market power cannot exist.[28] Furthermore, some deem it rather unlikely that Google has any incentive to extend its market power in "general search" into "specialized search" by ignoring consumer preferences (i.e. manipulating search results) and has no incentive to exclude specialized search providers.[29]

3.3.2 Multi-Sided Markets

A multi-sided market is generally defined as a platform to coordinate the demands of distinct groups of customers who need each other in some way.[30] Thus, an interdependent demand between these customer groups is required. On such markets two (or multiple) distinct groups of end-users exist, which benefit from

---

[26] *Evans/Noel,* Two-Sided Market Definition, in Evans (ed.) Platform Economics: Essays on Multi-Sided Businesses, Competition Policy International, 2011, at 148–150.

[27] Google's market share [U.S., July 2013] in general search: 67 % [Bing 18 %, Yahoo 11 %], see: http://www.comscore.com/Insights/Press_Releases/2013/8/comScore_Releases_July_2013_U.S._Search_Engine_Rankings (accessed 12 September 2013).

[28] *Bork/Sidak,* What Does the Chicago School Teach about Internet Search and the Antitrust Treatment of Google?, (2012) 8 Journal of Competition Law & Economics 663, at 675.

[29] *Bork/Sidak, supra* note 28, at 674 ff.

[30] *Evans/Noel,* Defining Markets that Involve Multi-Sided Platform Businesses: An Empirical Framework With an Application to Google's Purchase of DoubleClick (2007), at 3, available at: http://ssrn.com/abstract=1027933 (accessed 12 September 2013).

interacting through one or several common platforms.[31] The platform serves as a "matchmaker" to facilitate exchange between the customer groups. This reduces the transaction costs for the two customer groups to find each other and leads to "indirect network effects": the value that a customer on one side realizes increases with the number of customers on the other side.[32] Common examples of multi-sided markets or platforms are videogame platforms, payment systems, dating websites, application stores, and (other) online market places (like eBay).[33]

Applying these principles for multi-sided markets to search engines, relevant consumer groups are "search users" and "advertisers". The question is now whether or not an "interdependent demand" exists between these groups. In "general search" the search user has demand for (organic) search results and (general) information. In contrast, advertisers have demand for search users as (potential) customers. Since there is no interdependent demand between the customer groups "search user" and "advertiser", the general search market should rather not be considered as a multi-sided market. On the other hand, in "specialized (product) search", the search user needs specific product information and information on (potential) seller; the advertisers need search users as (potential) customers. Since one could conclude a possible interdependent demand between these customer groups, the specialized search market could be assessed as a multi-sided market. This conclusion could have significant importance for the market definition pursuant to the "SSNIP test" (see above). In this respect practicable principles for the application of this test need to be further identified and considered.

4 Summary

Several preliminary questions regarding the antitrust assessment of Google's business are still unsolved. The core issue is the definition of the relevant product market (or *markets*). In this respect, the specific characteristics of multi-sided markets will need to be taken into consideration. Regarding the *Google* investigation, it remains unclear which markets the FTC actually investigated (and with which results). Here too, the investigation did not bring any new findings for the antitrust enforcement in (multi-sided) online markets.

---

[31] *Rochet/Tirole*, Platform Competition in Two-Sided Markets, (2003) 1 Journal of the European Economic Association 990, at 990; *Evans/Schmalensee*, The Antitrust Analysis of Multi-Sided Platform Businesses, University of Chicago Institute for Law & Economics Olin Research Paper No. 623 (2013), at 2, available at: http://ssrn.com/abstract=2185373 (accessed 12 September 2013).

[32] *Evans*, Two-Sided Market Definition, in American Bar Association, Market Definition in Antitrust: Theory and Case Studies (2009), chapter XII, at 4; *Evans/Noel*, *supra* note 30, at 5–6.

[33] See e.g. *Rochet/Tirole*, *supra* note 31, at 990–993; *Rysman*, The Economics of Two-Sided Markets, (2009) 23(3) Journal of Economic Perspectives 125, at 125; *Evans*, Antitrust Economics of Two-Sided Markets, in Evans (ed.) Platform Economics: Essays on Multi-Sided Businesses, 2011, at 74–75.

Following the market definition as a very first step, issues like the following have to be addressed: Assuming Google has a dominant position in the general search market—did it actually tie its specialized search to its general search to foreclose competitors? Does Google control "superior resources" (such as user data or IT infrastructure) as an entry barrier to (potential) competitors? Do we conceivably need new tools to analyze market conditions and in particular market power in rapidly-evolving and constantly changing information markets? In the end, antitrust lawyers and economists are still facing the question how to enforce antitrust law in online markets the most effective way.

Discriminatory Conduct in the ICT Sector: A Legal Framework

Pablo Ibáñez Colomo

Abstract Vertical access disputes are frequent in the ICT sector. Prominent cases before the European Commission, such as *Google*, and some regulatory debates—and in particular discussions about "net neutrality"—are evidence of this. The purpose of this piece is to identify a legal framework for the assessment of unilateral discriminatory practices under competition law. Three main approaches could be considered: (1) a welfare-based approach, based alone on the economic impact of the practice on welfare; (2) an approach based on the (presumed or alleged) intent of the firm; and (3) one that seeks to achieve consistency by examining the substantive standards applying to similar practices. It is shown that the latter approach is to be preferred, as it seems to be not only sound from an economic perspective, but in line with the purpose and logic of competition law regimes.

1 Introduction

Vertical access disputes in the information and communication technology (hereinafter, "ICT") industries are frequent. In the field of competition law alone, we have recently witnessed controversies relating, inter alia, to the conditions of access to Microsoft's operating system,[1] to the conditions under which IBM supplies

---

[1] Commission Decision of 24 March 2004 relating to a proceeding under Article 82 of the EC Treaty (Case COMP/C-3/37.792 – *Microsoft*) (summary decision in [2007] OJ L 32/23) (hereinafter, *"Microsoft I"*) and Commission Decision of 16 December 2009 relating to a proceeding under Article 102 of the Treaty on the Functioning of the European Union and Article 54 of the EEA Agreement (Case COMP/39.530—*Microsoft (Tying)*) (summary decision in [2010] OJ C 36/7) (hereinafter, *"Microsoft II"*).

P. Ibáñez Colomo (✉)
Department of Law, London School of Economics and Political Science, London, UK
e-mail: P.Ibanez-Colomo@lse.ac.uk

inputs for the maintenance of its mainframe computers to third parties,[2] or to the use of non-proprietary software development tools in Apple's products.[3] At the time of writing, the single most significant pending case before the European Commission (hereinafter, the "Commission") originated following allegations that Google's search engine discriminates against competing services on vertically related segments of the value chain.[4]

Access issues in these industries are perceived to be so important that ad hoc regimes—typically, more severe and intrusive than general competition law provisions—have either been adopted or their adoption is or has been contemplated in the EU and the US. Regulation addressing the relationship between content producers and broadband Internet providers (which is generally debated under the label of "net neutrality") is probably the most prominent of these, but not the only one. During the past decade, the reach of intervention has expanded on markets related to, and around, the exploitation of electronic communications networks and services. For instance, the British communications regulator, Ofcom, imposed on the leading pay television provider in the UK an obligation to supply some of its premium channels to its downstream competitors.[5] In the Netherlands, cable television operators have been required by law to open their networks to third parties.[6]

The reasons behind the pervasiveness of vertical access disputes (and the resulting growth of, formal and informal, explicit and implicit, ad hoc responses) in ICT industries are relatively well identified. A major reason has to do with the fact that dominant positions, even quasi-monopolies, are not infrequent in innovation-intensive markets. Suffice it to think of the status of firms like Google, Intel or Microsoft in their core areas of activity. Such positions are sometimes the consequence of network effects, whereby the demand for a product increases along with the number of its users.[7] The cost structure of many ICT industries—and more precisely the fact that firms therein often face very high fixed costs and virtually

---

[2] Commission Decision of 13 December 2011 relating to proceedings under Article 102 of the Treaty on the Functioning of the European Union and Article 54 of the EEA Agreement (Case COMP/39.692—*IBM Maintenance Services*) (notified under document C(2011) 9245) (summary decision in [2012] OJ C 18/6).

[3] European Commission: "Statement on Apple's iPhone policy changes" (IP/10/1175, 25 September 2010).

[4] European Commission: "Antitrust: Commission probes allegations of antitrust violations by Google" (IP/10/1624, 30 November 2010). See also Case AT.39.740 – *Foundem v Google*, ongoing.

[5] Ofcom, *Pay TV Statement*, 31 March 2010, available at http://stakeholders.ofcom.org.uk/consultations/third_paytv/statement/.

[6] An (unofficial) translation of the relevant text can be found at http://www.government.nl/documents-and-publications/notes/2012/06/07/dutch-telecommunications-act.html. The text of the approved bill in the original language, including information about the legislative procedure followed, can be found at http://www.eerstekamer.nl.

[7] On the notion of network effects, see *Farrell/Klemperer*, Coordination and Lock-In: Competition with Switching Costs and Network Effects, in Armstrong/Porter, Handbook of Industrial Organization, vol 3, Amsterdam: Elsevier, 2007. As the authors explain, some markets subject to network effects may "tip" in favour of the larger network to the exclusion of competing ones.

insignificant marginal costs—is also conducive to market concentration.[8] A second fundamental reason is that vertical integration is common. For instance, Microsoft is active not only on the market for operating systems, but also on related markets for applications such as web browsers or media players. Likewise, Google offers e-mail, mapping and video services on top of its search engine. Whenever an instance of vertical integration coincides with a very strong position of dominance (or a quasi-monopoly) at at least one level of the value chain, claims that the vertically integrated firm uses its power on one market to favour its affiliated services on a related one seem inevitable.

The purpose of this contribution is to propose a framework for the assessment of instances of unilateral discrimination by a vertically integrated firm under EU competition law. Even though the question has a very high profile (it is for instance at the heart of the "net neutrality" debate) and has as a result been discussed very often, much confusion remains in relation to the principles that should apply to assess it in practice. As a result, the idea that differential treatment is problematic in and of itself is gaining acceptance among authorities, commentators and stakeholders. According to this view, the role of competition law would be to guarantee equal treatment to affiliated and non-affiliated divisions of the dominant firm.

The perception that EU competition law mandates a level playing field is probably the consequence of the influence of the ad hoc regimes with which it overlaps. The latter typically provide for unqualified access and non-discrimination obligations, the logic of which is not necessarily explained, and the consequences of which are not necessarily assessed systematically. This paper will show that, if anything, discrimination is very often (probably, more often than not) a manifestation of competition on the merits. In the same way that firms are, as a matter of principle, entitled to deal with whom they please, they should be entitled, as a matter of principle, to favour their affiliated divisions in vertical settings.

If one accepts the idea that discrimination is not as such problematic under EU competition law, it becomes necessary to identify a set of substantive principles defining the instances where the practice is anticompetitive and justifies remedial action. There are essentially two ways in which standards can be defined. One possible approach is to rely on a fully fledged balancing exercise to establish, on a case-by-case basis, whether the discriminatory conduct is detrimental to consumers and/or society. This is the approach that would be naturally favoured by economists, in that it acknowledges the fundamental principle whereby the effects of discrimination on welfare are ambiguous and therefore depend on the circumstances of the case. This approach reflects, it is submitted, a misunderstanding about the rationale of competition law. The purpose of competition law has never been to achieve optimal market outcomes, but to preserve the ability and the incentive of firms in the marketplace to outperform their rivals. If this simple—

---

[8] For an overview, see *Varian/Farrell/Shapiro*, The Economics of Information Technology – An Introduction, Cambridge University Press, 2004.

but fundamental—idea is taken into consideration, it becomes clear that an alternative approach should be favoured.

The definition of legal principles based on the logic underlying competition law demands the application of a consistent approach across the board, that is, that like situations be subject to the same substantive standards. It appears, from this perspective, that there is no reason to treat differently the various ways in which leveraging by vertically integrated firms may be manifested in the marketplace. The concern that discriminatory conduct leads to the elimination of rivals on a vertically related market is the same that exists when other practices (including, in particular, refusals to deal and "margin squeezes") are at stake. If so, it is necessary to apply a common set of conditions justifying intervention in all such instances. It would seem that, as a matter of principle, it is necessary to show, at the very least, that dealing with the vertically integrated firm is indispensable for its competitors on a related market.

After giving a definition of the problem, and explaining the different ways in which discrimination may be manifested in practice, this contribution examines the possible approaches that one could take to define the relevant legal principles. The third section considers the convenience of relying on a fully fledged economic approach, which, as explained above, would favour a case-by-case balancing of the welfare effects of the practice. The fourth section considers an approach based on the behaviour of the firm, that is, based on whether the observed discriminatory practice can be explained by anticompetitive intent. The final section is an attempt to identify some principles by analogy, that is, by examining how comparable practices are assessed from a legal standpoint.

2 Vertical Integration and Discrimination in ICT Industries

Where a firm is vertically integrated, and enjoys significant market power in at least one of the two markets in which it operates, it may use a variety of price and non-price mechanisms to harm its rivals—and thus leverage its position from one activity to another. The firm may simply decide to stop dealing with rivals, or supply (buy from) them on such conditions that make it impossible for them to operate at a profit. Other, more subtle, mechanisms—not leading to their immediate exclusion from the market—may be used by to discriminate against competing players. For instance, the vertically integrated firm may grant more favourable treatment to its affiliated division (supply under better conditions, supply higher quality products), or *vice versa*.

These strategies may be manifested in different ways in ICT industries. The administrative practice of the Commission provides several valuable examples in this sense. Interoperability, that is, the ability of complementary products to work together, is essential for programmers and application providers. Some cases relate to outright refusals to interoperate by a dominant firm. In 2004, the Commission found that Microsoft's withdrawal of the information necessary for the interoperability between its operating system (a market in which it holds a dominant position) and work group servers amounted to an abuse of dominance within the meaning of Article 102 TFEU.[9] In 2010, the Commission closed an investigation into Apple's practices relating to the licensing conditions imposed on third-party application developers. For the applications to run on its mobile phones, the firm required the use of its "native programming tools and approved languages", thereby excluding those of competitors, such as Adobe Flash.

There are other cases in which the concerns of the Commission did not relate to an outright refusal to interoperate, but to the degradation of the quality of the interoperability information provided to competitors. This was the key aspect in the *Intel/McAfee* merger, decided in 2011.[10] The Commission expressed concerns about the possibility that Intel, which enjoyed a very strong position on the market for microprocessors, would favour or penalise firms competing with McAfee for the development of security software products. Two main scenarios of discrimination were considered in the decision. First, it was feared that the merged entity could degrade the quality of the interoperability provided to rivals.[11] Secondly, the Commission expressed concerns about the possibility that McAfee would be technically tied to the microprocessors.[12] As a result, the operation was only cleared after Intel agreed to provide for remedies creating a level playing field on the market for security software. A similar scenario of discrimination was examined by the Commission in *Microsoft/Skype*.[13] In this case, the authority assessed, inter alia, whether, in the post-merger scenario, the entity resulting from the operation would have the incentive to degrade the quality of Skype when accessed by means of an operating system other than Windows.[14] Conversely, it considered whether Microsoft would degrade the quality of communication systems competing with Skype when accessed via Windows.[15]

Similar issues are at stake in the ongoing proceedings against Google. As mentioned in the introduction Google runs several vertically related services on top of its search engine. Some firms active on these neighbouring markets claimed that Google's affiliated services are unduly favoured in the search engine (they are presented at the top of the search page) and/or that rival services are demoted in the search list. This alleged practice was seen with concern by the Commission insofar

---

[9] *Microsoft I*, *supra* note 1.

[10] Commission Decision of 26 January 2011, *Intel/McAfee* (Case COMP/M.5984) [2011] OJ C 98/1.

[11] *Ibid.*, paras 128–174.

[12] *Ibid.*, paras 175–221.

[13] Commission Decision of 7 October 2011, *Microsoft/Skype* (Case COMP/M.6281) [2011] OJ C 341/2.

[14] *Ibid.*, paras 144–150.

[15] *Ibid.*, paras 151–158.

as it "unduly diverts traffic" away from these rival services and could as a consequence, as explained by Vice-President Almunia in a public speech, deprive consumers of search results that are more relevant for them.[16]

The abovementioned cases reproduce some concerns that have been commonly examined by the Commission in relation to the exploitation of communications networks. Following the liberalisation of these activities at the EU level, the authority has monitored closely whether the wholesale prices charged by vertically integrated incumbents are sufficient to allow its rivals to operate at a profit on downstream markets (broadband Internet services, voice telephony); that is, whether incumbents have engaged in a "margin squeeze".[17] The Commission has also examined non-price strategies whereby incumbents seek to obstruct the activities of new entrants for instance by imposing unreasonable conditions or delays when dealing with access requests.[18] It is only more recently that the authority has addressed through competition law the central concerns underlying the "net neutrality" debate. In July 2013, the Commission confirmed having conducted unannounced inspections at the premises of several telecommunications operators. While at the time of writing the authority had not taken further steps, it confirmed in a press release that discrimination against non-affiliated content providers is the concern that prompted the inspections.[19]

As can be seen from these examples, the Commission has regularly examined discrimination claims both under Article 102 TFEU and in the field of merger control. What is notable—and what explains the preparation of this piece—is that it is not entirely clear whether, and when, discrimination is likely to be an issue of concern when implemented by a dominant firm. While the Guidance on the application of Article 102 TFEU (hereinafter, the "Guidance Paper") suggests that the Commission is only likely to intervene where a unilateral practice is likely

---

[16] "Statement of VP Almunia on the Google antitrust investigation" (Speech/12/372, 21 May 2012) and "The Google antitrust case: what is at stake?" (Speech/13/768, 1 October 2013).

[17] See the definition of a "margin squeeze" provided in C-52/09, *Konkurrensverket v TeliaSonera Sverige AB* [2011] ECR I-527, para. 32: "there would be such a margin squeeze if, inter alia, the spread between the wholesale prices for ADSL input services and the retail prices for broadband connection services to end users were either negative or insufficient to cover the specific costs of the ADSL input services which TeliaSonera has to incur in order to supply its own retail services to end users, so that that spread does not allow a competitor which is as efficient as that undertaking to compete for the supply of those services to end users". The leading cases include Commission Decision of 21 May 2003 relating to a proceeding under Article 82 EC of the Treaty (Case COMP/C-1/37.451, 37.578, 37.579 – *Deutsche Telekom AG*) [2003] OJ L 263/9 and Commission Decision of 4 July 2007 relating to proceedings under Article 82 of the EC Treaty (Case COMP/38.784 – *Wanadoo España v Telefónica*) (summary decision in [2008] OJ C 83/6).

[18] Commission Decision of 22 June 2011 relating to a proceeding under Article 102 of the Treaty on the Functioning of the European Union (Case COMP/39.525 – *Telekomunikacja Polska*) (summary decision in [2011] OJ C 324/7).

[19] European Commission: "Commission confirms unannounced inspections in Internet connectivity services" (Memo/13/681, 11 July 2013).

to lead to market foreclosure,[20] the abovementioned cases fail to provide unequivocal answers as to whether, and to what extent, an analysis of the effects of discriminatory conduct is necessary to establish an abuse.

The absence of clear substantive principles is primarily due to the fact that there are few cases that spell out expressly the analytical framework applying to the assessment of the practice, as well as the reasons why it is a potential source of concerns in the first place. For instance, the investigation in the Apple case was closed once the firm announced a change in its policy that addressed the concerns expressed by the authority, and the concise press release issued by the Commission remained elliptic on the applicable substantive principles. Similarly, the authority has, in the recent past, repeatedly—and publicly—invited Google to submit commitments addressing the potentially anticompetitive practices identified following a preliminary assessment.[21] However, it has never explained or clarified the reasons why the practices at stake in the case are deemed potentially problematic from a legal standpoint. It is against this vacuum that the discussion of the different substantive approaches to the question becomes relevant.

3 A Welfare-Based Approach for the Assessment of Discrimination

The starting point of a purely economic approach to the definition of substantive standards is typically an assessment of the plausible welfare effects of the practice under examination. This preliminary step is necessary insofar as the vast majority of potentially anticompetitive practices—and discrimination by vertically integrated firms is not an exception in this regard—have ambiguous effects on welfare. The question of whether they are positive or negative for consumers and/or society as a whole is established on the basis of a fact-specific balancing exercise that evaluates whether, in the market context in which the practice is implemented, the potential gains to which it may lead are likely to weigh more than any negative effects.

Any case-by-case assessment revolves around a theory of harm—that is, of a *story* explaining the mechanism through which any negative effects would be

---

[20] Guidance on the Commission's enforcement priorities in applying Article 82 of the EC Treaty to abusive exclusionary conduct by dominant undertakings, [2009] OJ C 45/7 (hereinafter, the "Guidance Paper"), paras 19–20.

[21] On 21 May 2012, Commissioner Almunia stated the following: "If Google comes up with an outline of remedies which are capable of addressing our concerns, I will instruct my staff to initiate the discussions in order to finalise a remedies package. This would allow to solve our concerns by means of a commitment decision – pursuant to Article 9 of the EU Antitrust Regulation – instead of having to pursue formal proceedings with a Statement of objections and to adopt a decision imposing fines and remedies". ("Statement of VP Almunia on the Google antitrust investigation" (Speech/12/372, 21 May 2012)).

manifested, and the reasons why such an outcome is a plausible one. A theory of harm comprises three distinct steps. As far as discrimination is concerned, it would be necessary to show, first, that the vertically integrated firm has the *ability* to harm competition on a market neighbouring the one in which it holds a dominant position (the question would be, for instance, whether a dominant upstream supplier has the means to foreclose its rivals on the downstream market for the distribution of the goods). This question depends on the features of the relevant markets (whether they are closely related or there are overlaps between the two, whether the input supplied upstream is qualitatively or quantitatively important for competition downstream), and on the degree of dominance enjoyed by the firm on the market in which it holds a dominant position.[22] Following this assessment, it is necessary to show, as a second step, that the firm in question has the *incentive* to favour its affiliated division.[23] This will be typically the case, for instance, where it is likely to capture the demand away from its rivals, or where there are greater profits to be made on the neighbouring market where the firm seeks to extend its dominant position.

The balancing exercise of the overall impact of discrimination takes place as the following and last step. Even if it is established that the vertically integrated firm has both the ability and the incentive to foreclose competition on a neighbouring market, a discrimination strategy that seeks to harm its rivals may not necessarily be harmful for competition and/or consumers. It may be the case, for instance, that rivals on the neighbouring market have the means to deploy counterstrategies to reduce their economic dependence on the vertically integrated firm.[24] In some cases, the efficiency gains resulting from the integration of two activities are so important that they are sufficient to outweigh any potential negative effects.[25]

This approach, while—in principle—sound from an economic perspective, is not obvious to implement in practice. Legal certainty requires that firms know in advance whether their conduct is likely to raise concerns. It is difficult to see how this certainty can be guaranteed where administrative action depends on a case-by-case assessment. In other words—and to the extent that competition policy is enforced by means of legal provisions—this approach to enforcement is very difficult—arguably impossible—to implement. This means that it would be necessary to provide, at the very least, a set of proxies (what economists sometimes call a "structured rule of reason") that make it possible for stakeholders to anticipate the instances in which intervention is likely. An example in this regard is provided by

---

[22] See, by analogy, the Guidelines on the assessment of non-horizontal mergers under the Council Regulation on the control of concentrations between undertakings, [2008] OJ C 265/6 (hereinafter, the "Non-Horizontal Merger Guidelines"), paras 33–39.

[23] *Ibid.*, by analogy, paras 40–46.

[24] *Ibid.*, para. 39: "In its assessment, the Commission will consider, on the basis of the information available, whether there are effective and timely counter-strategies that the rival firms would be likely to deploy. Such counterstrategies include the possibility of changing their production process so as to be less reliant on the input concerned or sponsoring the entry of new suppliers upstream".

[25] *Ibid.*, para. 52.

the Guidelines on non-horizontal mergers, which evaluates very similar issues (and in particular the fact that a vertical merger leads to the foreclosure of the upstream or downstream markets involved in the operation).

Another aspect that one should not ignore and that is equally crucial is the economic impact on legal uncertainty that a pure case-by-case model would have. Absent clear *ex ante* principles for the assessment of discriminatory practices, firms may be reluctant to start dealing with downstream rivals so as to avoid subsequent claims of anticompetitive discrimination. If this is so, a substantive standard based on a pure *ex post* economic assessment would have a negative impact on the competitive process, contrary to what it is meant to achieve. This is a concern that has influenced the definition of legal principles around, for instance, the licensing of technology. The current approach of the Commission to the matter is crucially based on the principle that a restrictive licence is to be preferred—insofar as it is more conducive to competition and is more beneficial for consumers—than a decision not to license in the first place.[26] In this same vein, uncertainty about the imposition of a duty to deal with rivals on non-discriminatory terms may have a negative impact on firms' incentives to invest and develop new products. This second aspect is explored at length below.

A more fundamental objection to a welfare-based approach to the definition of substantive standards relates to the fact that it probably sits at odds with the logic and rationale of the discipline. If enforcement is agnostic about market structures, in the sense that interference with existing structures is deemed justified whenever intervention is expected to yield superior outcomes, remedial action is likely to go beyond the limits that would logically derive from EU competition law. Take the assessment of refusals to deal as an example illustrating this idea. As will be examined in greater detail below, an analysis of the case law unambiguously shows that the question of whether a refusal is abusive does not depend on a balancing exercise aimed to establish whether the position of consumers and competition would improve following the imposition of an obligation to supply.[27] In fact, the ECJ has clarified that such an obligation is only imposed in "exceptional circumstances" that are notoriously difficult to meet in practice. This is so because competition law takes, as a matter of principle, market structures as a given, not as a variable that may be altered or fine-tuned in an attempt to achieve optimal welfare outcomes. Accordingly, competition law can be said to be systematically under-enforced. Outcomes that would be sub-optimal from an economic standpoint are indeed perceived to be an integral and necessary consequence of a workable competition law regime.[28]

---

[26] For a discussion of this matter, see *Korah*, Draft block exemption for technology transfer, (2004) 25 European Competition Law Review 247.

[27] The Commission, however, seemed to move in that direction in the *Microsoft I* case, which was validated by the General Court when challenged. See Case T-201/04, *Microsoft Corp. v Commission*, [2007] ECR II-3601, and in particular paras 621–665.

[28] For a discussion of this matter, see in particular *Hovenkamp*, The Antitrust Enterprise – Principle and Execution, Harvard University Press, 2005, pp. 45–56.

4 Using Firm Motivations as an Analytical Benchmark

4.1 Assuming Intent

A second alternative to the definition of substantive standards would be based not so much on the overall impact of the practice on competition and consumers, but on the motivations behind its adoption by the vertically integrated firm. In other words, competition law would come into play where there is evidence showing that the firm has purportedly engaged in the conduct with a view to eliminating its rivals. Substantive standards based on the (actual or presumed) subjective intent of the vertically integrated firm can be defined in several ways. One possibility is to establish a rebuttable presumption pursuant to which favouring an affiliated division (or discriminating against unaffiliated rivals on a neighbouring market) is based on anticompetitive intent. Accordingly, the conduct will be found to be abusive unless the dominant firm is able to provide an objective justification for the differential treatment. To the extent that the affiliated division of the dominant firm and its rivals are in comparable positions, this approach is not entirely unreasonable. What is more, it finds some support in the letter of Article 102 (c) TFEU, whereby the application of "dissimilar conditions to equivalent transactions with other trading parties" is abusive—and this insofar as it leads to a "competitive disadvantage".

Competition authorities and review courts have learned over the past decades that one needs to be extremely careful when inferring anticompetitive intent from a particular practice. Sometimes, what looks like a one-dimensional device the only purpose of which is to eliminate rivals is, upon closer scrutiny, a subtle way to promote competition and to improve consumer welfare. It is simply incorrect to presume anticompetitive intent whenever a particular practice is a plausible means for the firm to achieve efficiency gains. For instance, it is now clear that the reasons why a firm active on two or more closely related markets may engage in tying or bundling often have little to do with the elimination of rivals, but with the synergies and cost savings that derive from the common sale of two products. If this is so, assuming anticompetitive motivations without evaluating the plausibility of alternative explanations—and, by the same token, prohibiting differential treatment *prima facie*—would not only be problematic from a legal standpoint, but would also penalise consumers and the economy as a whole without valid reason. In this sense, it is not surprising that the Commission, in the Guidance Paper, emphasises the efficiency gains that may result from the practices it addresses.[29] It is equally unsurprising that enforcement priorities are defined in the document not by

---

[29] See in particular the following: In para. 34 of the Guidance Paper (*supra* note 20), the Commission explains that "[i]n order to convince customers to accept exclusive purchasing obligations, the dominant undertaking may have to compensate them, in whole or in part, for the loss in competition resulting from the exclusivity. Where such compensation is given, it may be in the individual interest of a customer to enter into an exclusive purchasing obligation with the dominant

reference to the dominant firm's intent but by reference, as mentioned above, to the likely impact of the practice on its rivals' ability and incentive to compete.

The attitude of the US Federal Trade Commission ("FTC") in the proceedings opened against Google illustrates this idea particularly well. Alongside the Commission, the FTC examined claims that Google's Universal Search, whereby general search results are presented in combination with its affiliated specialised services, which are displayed prominently on top of the search list, is anticompetitive. Even though it is difficult to question or dispute in this particular case that Google gives differential treatment to its own services, the agency decided not to take action against the firm. Instead of assuming anticompetitive motivations in Google's policy, the FTC noted that the prominence given to its affiliated services was positive for consumers. As a result, the practice may be plausibly interpreted as an attempt to make search results more relevant and accurate.[30]

4.2 Establishing Intent on a Case-by-Case Basis

A second possibility is to establish intent on a case-by-case basis, that is, to determine whether the difference in treatment between affiliated and non-affiliated firms is the consequence of a deliberate plan to eliminate a competitor. Reliance on the intent of the vertically integrated firm raises a number of complex issues. The most immediate question one should ask is whether there is basis in the case law for intervention based on subjective considerations alone. There should be little doubt, in light of the case law of the ECJ, that intent is a factor that may be considered in the overall assessment of the abusive nature of a particular line of conduct.[31] This is a factor that is crucial to make sense of some ECJ rulings, and that can play a role in borderline scenarios, as is the case where a dominant firm prices below average total costs.[32] It is equally clear from the case law, however, that the notion of abuse is an objective one.[33] Accordingly, it would seem that at least a modicum of effects is necessary to take action and, by the same token, that intent alone is insufficient to take action. In fact, Article 102(c) TFEU

---

undertaking". Similarly, in para. 49, it states that "[t]ying and bundling are common practices intended to provide customers with better products or offerings in more cost effective ways".

[30] "Google Agrees to Change Its Business Practices to Resolve FTC Competition Concerns In the Markets for Devices Like Smart Phones, Games and Tablets, and in Online Search" (3 January 2013), available at http://www.ftc.gov/opa/2013/01/google.shtm. The FTC explained "that the introduction of Universal Search, as well as additional changes made to Google's search algohrithms – even those that may have had the effect of harming individual competitors – could be plausibly justified as innovations that improved Google's product and the experience of its users. It therefore has chosen to close the investigation".

[31] Case C-549/10 P, *Tomra Systems ASA and others v Commission*, judgment of 19 April 2012, not yet reported, para. 21.

[32] Case C-62/86, *AKZO Chemie BV v Commission* [1991] ECR I-3359, para. 72.

[33] Case 85/76, *Hoffmann-La Roche & Co. AG v Commission*, [1979] ECR 461, para. 91.

provides that discriminatory conduct must impose a "competitive disadvantage" on firms for it to be abusive. It is true at the same time that, as far as many practices are concerned, this threshold of effects is a very low one that can be easily met by an authority or a claimant.

More relevant is probably the question of whether intent should be a relevant factor in the analysis. In this regard, there is much literature casting doubt on the pertinence of the criterion when drawing the line between pro- and anticompetitive behaviour. Competition law seeks to preserve firms' ability and incentive to outperform their rivals in the marketplace. If this is so, evidence showing that the firm was trying to eliminate a rival can be interpreted as meaning that the market is fiercely competitive, and that no intervention is necessary as a result. In this same vein, there seems to be no reason to take action—even if anticompetitive intent can be unequivocally established—where the firm that was trying to eliminate a competitor does not succeed in its attempt.

Coming back to the objectives of competition law, the single most important problem with relying on intent as an indicator of anticompetitive conduct relates to the fact that it implies that dominant firms are, as a matter of principle, under a duty to deal with their rivals on a non-discriminatory basis. The problem with this idea is, first of all, one of consistency in the enforcement of the law. As mentioned above, firms are in principle entitled to deal with whom they please under competition law, and this is also true of dominant undertakings within the meaning of Article 102 TFEU. Even though such a refusal can only amount to an abuse in "exceptional circumstances", it seems obvious that it is always, or almost always motivated by an attempt to exclude a competitor, or to prevent it from becoming a credible one. Where a firm refuses to deal with a rival, it indeed does so in order to retain a competitive advantage as a means to outperform it. It is difficult to see why this reasoning would be accepted without serious controversy in the context of one practice, but not in the context of another practice that is nothing but a different, more subtle, way to achieve the same objective.

A second fundamental issue relates to the reasons why a duty to deal is exceptional in competition law. If the threshold for forcing firms to supply their rivals were to be set at a relatively low level, intervention may end up harming their incentives to outperform one another, harming the competitive process (at least from a long-run perspective) as a result. As explained by Advocate General Jacobs in *Bronner*,[34] firms are likely to lose their incentives to invest and innovate if they are unable to exploit their competitive advantages at will. By the same token, other firms may choose to rely on competition law to gain access to their competitors' advantages instead of investing themselves in the improvement of their products or services. Mandating the creation of a level playing field by means of strict

---

[34] Opinion of Advocate General Jacobs in Case C-7/97, *Oscar Bronner GmbH & Co. KG v Mediaprint Zeitungs- und Zeitschriftenverlag GmbH & Co. KG, Mediaprint Zeitungsvertriebsgesellschaft mbH & Co. KG and Mediaprint Anzeigengesellschaft mbH & Co. KG,* [1998] ECR I-7791.

non-discrimination obligations could have exactly the same (negative) effects on incentives as a duty to deal imposed liberally or across the board. If so, there is every reason to treat the remedy with the same caution, and to avoid intent-based considerations when establishing the circumstances in which a duty to deal is abusive. Put differently, it should be *prima facie* valid for a vertically integrated firm to claim that it treats an affiliated division more favourably because it is trying to preserve its competitive advantage.

5 Towards Across-the-Board Consistency

The fundamental lesson one can draw from the discussion above is that, in the same way that they are entitled, as a matter of principle, to deal with whom they please, firms should be, as a rule, entitled to discriminate in favour of their affiliated services. Accordingly, it is only in a restrictive set of "exceptional circumstances" that the creation of a level playing field should be mandated under competition law. The fact that this may occasionally (even regularly) lead to false negatives is not a relevant factor in the analysis. Similarly, and in the same way that intent-based considerations are not taken into account when determining whether a refusal to deal is abusive, they should not influence the legal assessment when discriminatory conduct by a vertically integrated firm is at stake.

Consistency would require that the case law on refusals to deal, as laid down in *Magill*, *Bronner* and *IMS Health* extends to the application of "dissimilar conditions". Accordingly, it would be necessary to establish, at the very least, that it is indispensable for rivals at either level of the value chain to deal with the vertically integrated dominant firm. This means, as explained by the ECJ in *IMS Health*, examining whether "there are products or services which constitute alternative solutions, even if they are less advantageous, and whether there are technical, legal or economic obstacles capable of making it impossible or at least unreasonably difficult for any undertaking seeking to operate in the market".[35] The "indispensability" requirement is a logical corollary to another condition set out in *Magill* whereby it is necessary to show that the refusal leads to the elimination of "all competition" on the relevant downstream market.[36] The threshold for intervention resulting for this line of case law is very difficult to meet in practice, and, in line with the above, rests on the presumption that allowing vertically integrated firms to exploit their property at will is generally pro-competitive.

While this looks like the most straightforward solution, it is necessary to take into consideration the fact that the case law of the ECJ has not always reflected a

---

[35] Case C-418/01, *IMS Health GmbH & Co. OHG v NDC Health GmbH & Co. KG*, [2004] ECR I-5039, para. 28.
[36] Joined Cases C-241/91 P and C-242/91 P, *Radio Telefis Eireann (RTE) and Independent Television Publications Ltd (ITP) v Commission ("Magill")*, [1995] ECR I-743, para. 56.

similar concern with consistency when setting out the substantive standards applying to a particular practice. This fact became clearly apparent in the *TeliaSonera* case, where the ECJ was invited to rule on the conditions under which a "margin squeeze" is abusive under Article 102 TFEU. The fundamental point related to whether it is necessary to establish, as a pre-condition for intervention, that dealing with the vertically integrated firm is "indispensable" within the meaning of *Magill* and *IMS Health*. It is out of a concern with consistency that this issue was raised. If the vertically integrated firm would not abuse its dominant position by refusing to deal with its downstream rivals, there seems to be no reason why it should not be entitled to deal with them on conditions that do not allow them to operate at a profit on the downstream market (that is, *qui potest majus, potest et minus*). The ECJ rejected this argument, and held that a "margin squeeze" may be abusive even when the vertically integrated firm would not have been under a duty to start dealing with its downstream rivals. When coming to this conclusion, the ECJ emphasised the importance of preserving the "effectiveness" of Article 102 TFEU.[37] Thus consistency across practices that are essentially similar ways to achieve leveraging was given less weight than the leeway of the Commission to take action in a broad range of scenarios.

Interestingly, the Commission endorsed the opposite approach in the Guidance Paper. In that document, the authority commits to treat refusal-to-deal cases and margin-squeeze cases under a common set of principles, which comprise establishing that access is indispensable (or "objectively necessary",[38] which is the expression used by the Commission) and that it leads to the elimination of all competition ("elimination of effective competition"[39]). According to the logic of the Guidance Paper, the *TeliaSonera* judgment was correctly decided, but for reasons other than those explicitly relied upon by the ECJ. The Commission found it appropriate to relax the conditions under which a duty to deal may be imposed where (1) there is a regulatory regime already in place forcing the vertically integrated firm to deal with rivals and/or (2) the competitive advantage enjoyed by the vertically integrated firm is the consequence of state involvement, either through the grant of subsidies or the award of exclusive or special rights. The Commission assumes that in these two instances (which are typically present, often in a cumulative manner, where practices adopted by incumbent firms in recently liberalised industries, including TeliaSonera, are at stake) firms' incentives to invest and innovate are not jeopardised through the application of competition law.[40]

---

[37] *TeliaSonera*, *supra* note 17, para. 58: "if *Bronner* were to be interpreted otherwise, in the way advocated by TeliaSonera, that would, as submitted by the European Commission, amount to a requirement that before any conduct of a dominant undertaking in relation to its terms of trade could be regarded as abusive the conditions to be met to establish that there was a refusal to supply would in every case have to be satisfied, and that would unduly reduce the effectiveness of Article 102 TFEU".

[38] Guidance Paper, *supra* note 20, paras 83–84.

[39] *Ibid.*, para. 85.

[40] *Ibid.*, para. 82.

The very limited number of cases revolving primarily around exclusionary discrimination claims suggests in fact that the Commission acknowledges the risks of mandating the creation of a level playing field in circumstances that are not exceptional. In a sense, one could very well claim that the principles set out in the Guidance Paper were already present—albeit in implicit form—in its practice. Decisions like *Deutsche Bahn* and *Deutsche Post*, for instance, relate to practices by incumbent firms in a recently liberalised market.[41] The same can be said of a long line of commitment decisions adopted during the late 2000s concerning practices in energy-related markets (gas and electricity).[42] Outside these cases, it would seem that evidence of the "indispensability" of the input has been a pre-requisite for intervention. In *Clearstream*, for instance, the Commission claimed that the vertically integrated firm was an unavoidable trading partner and that it was not likely to expect the entry of a rival in the foreseeable future.[43] *IBM*, which related to the conditions under which the firm supplied inputs for the maintenance of its mainframe computers to third parties, was closed with commitments. However, the Commission claimed in the decision that it would have been able to show that dealing with IBM was indispensable for downstream firms.[44]

The *Google* case provides a valuable opportunity for the Commission to clarify the legal status of discriminatory practices. Unfortunately, however, nothing in the publicly available documents suggests that the authority finds it necessary to take action against the firm because it is indispensable for its rivals to be listed in the search engine. Likewise, nothing in these statements suggests that the alleged discrimination in the presentation of the results is deemed problematic insofar as it is tantamount to a refusal to deal within the meaning of the relevant case law.

---

[41] 94/210/EC: Commission Decision of 29 March 1994 relating to a proceeding pursuant to Articles 85 and 86 of the EC Treaty (IV/33.941 – HOV SVZ/MCN) [1994] OJ L 104/34 and 2001/892/EC: Commission Decision of 25 July 2001 relating to a proceeding under Article 82 of the EC Treaty (COMP/C-1/36.915 – *Deutsche Post AG – Interception of cross-border mail*) [2001] OJ L 331/40.

[42] See in particular Commission Decision of 3 December 2009 relating to a proceeding under Article 102 of the Treaty on the Functioning of the European Union and Article 54 of the EEA Agreement (Case COMP/39.316 – *GDF*) (summary decision in [2010] OJ C 57/13); Commission Decision of 4 May 2010 relating to a proceeding under Article 102 of the Treaty on the Functioning of the European Union and Article 54 of the EEA Agreement (Case COMP/39.317 – *E.ON Gas*) (summary decision in [2010] OJ C 278/9); and Commission Decision of 29 September 2010 relating to a proceeding under Article 102 of the Treaty on the Functioning of the European Union and Article 54 of the EEA Agreement (Case COMP/39.315 – *ENI*) (summary decision in [2010] OJ C 352/8). In these cases, the Commission emphasised the fact that access to the facilities owned by the incumbents was indispensable for competition to emerge or be sustained on vertically related markets.

[43] Commission Decision of 2 June 2004 relating to a proceeding under Article 82 of the EC Treaty (Case COMP/38.096—*Clearstream (Clearing and Settlement)*) (summary decision in [2009] OJ C 165/7).

[44] Commission decision of 13 December 2011 relating to a proceeding under Article 102 of the Treaty on the Functioning of the European Union and Article 54 of the EEA Agreement (Case COMP/39.692 – *IBM Maintenance Services*) (summary decision in [2012] OJ C 18/6), para. 38.

Ideally, the Commission should clarify in the decision putting an end to these proceedings the substantive standards under which Google's alleged practices have been assessed.

If the administrative action in the *Google* case is not based on the alleged indispensability of the search engine, but on other factors (whether they are intent or welfare-based), one would expect the Commission to explain why it endorses a different substantive standard in an instance that is materially similar to refusals to deal and to "margin squeeze" abuses. One should bear in mind in this regard that the adoption of the Guidance Paper is the consequence of the fact that the case law in the field of Article 102 TFEU in the mid-2000s grew confusing and unpredictable. In this sense, the fundamental goal of the document was not (contrary to what is often assumed) to advance what has come to be known as the "more economics-based approach", but to provide certainty about the enforcement approach that the Commission is likely to follow. If subsequent intervention becomes difficult to reconcile with the rationale underlying the Guidance Paper, then it is difficult to see the purpose that this soft-law instrument may have served.

If the Commission believes it is justified to relax the substantive standards applying to discrimination, it should draw an adequate line between lawful and unlawful forms of discrimination under Article 102 TFEU. One would logically expect that the authority would endorse, in such a case, the test of "anticompetitive foreclosure" that has become a gold standard in EU competition policy over the past years.[45] In addition, the Commission needs to explain how it intends to carve out discrimination as a stand-alone category of abusive conduct. One cannot ignore in this regard that the line between discriminatory practices and refusals to deal may not be easy to define in practice. At the very least, it seems that a case that would otherwise be framed as a refusal to deal can be easily converted into a claim of discrimination (one can easily claim in this sense that the refusal to share a competitive advantage amounts to applying dissimilar conditions to equivalent transactions within the meaning of Article 102(c) TFEU).

6 Conclusions

Claims that players in ICT industries discriminate against their rivals by favouring their own affiliated divisions are very frequent. The temptation to ban such practices and to impose a level playing field across the board is natural and as such unavoidable. Where a firm treats its own activities more favourably than those of a competitor, it is intuitively sound to jump to the conclusion that the practice should

---

[45] By the same token, and as far as price-based discrimination is concerned, one would expect the authority to endorse the "as efficient" competitor standard that is presented in para. 23 of the Guidance Paper, *supra* note 20 ("the Commission will normally only intervene where the conduct concerned has already been or is capable of hampering competition from competitors which are considered to be as efficient as the dominant undertaking").

be prohibited as the expression of exclusionary intent. This is all the more so when such practices are implemented by firms enjoying very large market shares—a far from unusual phenomenon in ICT industries. As a result, it is inevitable that such intuitions find their way into legislative regimes—some of which are an ad hoc reaction to very specific concerns—or into the way in which competition law is interpreted and enforced.

A fundamental conclusion following from this chapter is that for a firm to discriminate in favour of its own activities is, as a matter of principle, not contrary to the logic of EU competition law. If anything, it is consistent with the primary purpose of the discipline, which is to provide and preserve the ability and the incentive of firms to outperform one another in the marketplace. If it is true that firms are entitled, absent "exceptional circumstances", to deal with whom they please under Article 102 TFEU, it must be the case that they are entitled to favour, as a matter of principle, their own activities over those of rivals. This insight also sheds light on the availability of intent as a benchmark to identify the instances in which discrimination is abusive. There should be nothing anticompetitive as such in firms' attempts to exploit their competitive advantages in a way that leads to a more favourable treatment of affiliated activities.

The following conclusions can be inferred from the discussion above. First, any substantive standards establishing the abusive nature of discrimination by vertically integrated firms should take into account the need to preserve legal certainty. Firms' incentives to invest and innovate, and firms' willingness to deal with their rivals, may be negatively affected (harming competition as a result) where the principles applying to a particular practice remain unclear. Secondly, substantive standards must be defined with legal consistency in mind. Practices that are not fundamentally different from discrimination by vertically integrated firms (and in particular refusals to deal) should not be subject to different standards. As a result, there seems to be no reason to intervene in discrimination cases if there is not, at the very least, evidence that dealing with the vertically integrated firm is "indispensable" within the meaning of *Magill* and *Bronner*.

Competition Concerns in Multi-Sided Markets in Mobile Communication

Jonas Severin Frank

1 Introduction

The market for modern mobile phones (known as smartphones[1]) is growing.[2] Due to ongoing technical progress, these devices offer more and more functionality.[3] The possibility of an advanced use of the mobile internet is a key characteristic shared by most of them. The applications and services of these devices are built upon mobile operating systems[4] that allow the users to (partly) adjust the interface

---

[1] Smartphones can be defined as "wireless phones with advanced Internet browsing and application capabilities" in contrast to "Basic phones [which] are used primarily for calls and text messaging" [and] "Feature phones [which] are wireless phones with limited Internet browsing and application capabilities" (Commission decision of 13 February 2012, Case No COMP/M.6381 - Google/Motorola Mobility, at para. 13, footnote 13).

[2] Gartner (2014): Gartner Says Annual Smartphone Sales Surpassed Sales of Feature Phones for the First Time in 2013, Press Release, Egham, UK, 13 February 2014, available at: http://www.gartner.com/newsroom/id/2665715 (accessed 23 June 2014).

[3] Hahn/Singer, Smartphone Wars, (2010) The Milken Institute Review, First Quarter 52, at 54.

[4] "The mobile OS is a key part of the mobile software platform. An OS is 'system software' which controls the basic functions of an electronic device (mainly PCs, smartphones and tablets) and enables the user to make use of such an electronic device and run application software on it. Applications written for a given mobile OS will typically run on any mobile device using the same mobile OS, regardless of the manufacturer." Commission Decision, *Google/Motorola Mobility*, *supra* note 1, at para. 22, citing Case COMP/C-3/37.792 – *Microsoft*, Commission decision of 24 March 2004, para. 37 and Case COMP/M.6281 – *Microsoft/Skype*, Commission decision of 7 October 2011, para. 38.

J.S. Frank (✉)
Faculty of Business Administration and Economics, Economic Policy, Philipps-Universität Marburg, Germany
e-mail: severin.frank@wiwi.uni-marburg.de

to their preferences (e.g. customization by downloading applications). Within the value chain different players can be distinguished that are influencing the overall user experience of mobile handsets, i.e. manufacturers of mobile devices (e.g. Nokia, Apple, Samsung), hardware suppliers (e.g. chip developers), network carriers (e.g. Deutsche Telekom, Telefónica, Vodafone, Verizon), providers of mobile operating systems (e.g. Apple, Google), providers of mobile application stores (e.g. Apple, Google, Amazon) as well as providers of applications that are sold via mobile application stores (various players in a variety of fields like games, navigation, information, communication).

Thus, markets in mobile communication have a vertical structure.[5] Players who are active in this field are mostly vertically integrated, which becomes obvious in cases of companies like Google (until recently active in the fields of manufacturing of smartphones through its division Motorola Mobility,[6] internet network services in some regions in the US,[7] its mobile operating system Android, the mobile content store Google Play and applications like Gmail, Google Maps, Google Music, YouTube and more) or Apple (active in the fields of manufacturing of smartphones, the mobile operating system iOS, the mobile content store App Store and applications like iMovie, iPhoto, iBooks, iTunes and others). Similarly, companies like Samsung, Nokia, Microsoft or Blackberry (formerly Research in Motion) are active in several areas of this vertical value chain.[8]

In this paper a special focus is laid on the market for operating systems for mobile devices, i.e. smartphones. It should be noted that providers of mobile operating systems (MOS) can also be seen as input providers for the downstream market for mobile handsets.[9] MOSs have a particular importance for the decision of consumers to purchase a smartphone. Moreover, as the mobile operating system strongly influences whether and how applications can be accessed and how they ultimately run on the device, this importance even increases.[10] From a competition policy perspective interesting questions occur concerning market structure and

---

[5] However, the market delineation is not entirely clear; this is discussed below.

[6] Google merged with Motorola Mobility in 2011, but entered into an agreement to sell the company to Lenovo in early 2014; for more information see Google, Press Release, 15 August 2011, available at: http://investor.google.com/releases/2011/0815.html, and Google, Press Release, 29 January 2014, available at: http://investor.google.com/releases/2014/0129.html (accessed 27 February 2014).

[7] For more information see *Talbot*, Google's Internet Service Might Actually Bring the U.S. Up to Speed, MIT Technology Review (19 November 2012), available at: http://www.technologyreview.com/news/507476/googles-internet-service-might-actually-bring-the-us-up-to-speed/ (accessed 27 February 2014).

[8] *Kenney/Pon*, Structuring the Smartphone Industry: Is the Mobile Internet OS Platform the Key?, (2011) 11 Journal of Industry, Competition and Trade 239, at 245.

[9] Commission Decision, *Google/Motorola Mobility*, *supra* note 1, at para. 73.

[10] *Ibid.*, at para. 83.

characteristics as well as firms' behavior. The reason why it is worthwhile to specifically observe the market for MOSs is because there is a clear indication for a trend toward duopoly between Google's MOS Android and Apple's iOS, which results in potentially problematic outcomes. The two largest players in the market for the manufacturing of smartphones (in 2013 market share for Samsung was 31,0 %, for Apple -15,6 %) face competition through multiple vendors that seems to remain rather constant in comparison with figures from 2012 (in 2012 market share for Samsung was 30,3 %, for Apple -19,1 %).[11] Contrary to that, figures for MOSs indicate that the combined market shares of Google Android and Apple iOS lie at 94% (2013: Android 78,4 %, iOS 15,6 %) with an increasing trend (2012: Android 66,4 %, iOS 19,1 %).[12]

If the market for MOSs is on the brink of becoming a duopoly, it is relevant to ask to what extent this influences related markets and whether there is harm to future contestability. The question arises whether actual or potential competition is a sufficient constraint regarding abusive conduct of dominant firms or whether these firms have the ability and/or the incentive to discriminate against potential or actual competitors and consumers, especially taking into account that they are vertically integrated.[13] Before answering these questions it is necessary to discuss the characteristics of the market for MOSs (and its interplay with related markets) from a general perspective.

---

[11] Gartner, *supra* note 2.

[12] *Ibid*. Figures from 1Q14 indicate that the market share of Android is at 80 % (ABIresearch, Q1 2014 Smartphone OS Results: Android Dominates High Growth Developing Markets, Research News, London, United Kingdom, 6 May 2014, available at: https://www.abiresearch.com/press/q1-2014-smartphone-os-results-android-dominates-hi (accessed 23 June 2014)).

[13] In the European Commission's Guidelines on the assessment of non-horizontal mergers it is stated that "a non-horizontal merger may change the ability and incentive to compete on the part of the merging companies and their competitors in ways that cause harm to consumers." (Guidelines on the assessment of non-horizontal mergers under the Council Regulation on the control of concentrations between undertakings, [2008] OJ C 265/6, at para. 15). In this respect having the ability to engage in anticompetitive conduct refers to the question whether a company has the mere possibility to engage in specific conduct whereas the incentive to do so refers to the subsequent question of whether there exist constraining or countervailing incentive-based factors which might hinder the actual exploitation of abilities to discriminate (e.g. a firm could be able to discriminate against competitors by offering inferior support/denying access to an MOS, but does not have an incentive to do so if advertising revenues depend on competitors having access) (e.g. Commission Decision, *Google/Motorola Mobility*, *supra* note 1, at paras 86–94).

2 Mobile Communication Markets as Multi-Sided Platforms

Multi-sided markets are a well-described phenomenon and can be observed in diverse fields and areas.[14] They can be described by the existence of multiple customer groups (which may be sellers or buyers), the existence of some kind of connection between them referring to (multi-sided) indirect network externalities[15] and the need to resolve the problem of internalization of these indirect network externalities by an intermediary.[16] The underlying principle of indirect network externalities is that the utility for a customer on one market *indirectly* increases if the overall number of customers in the same market grows. Thus, markets, which can be seen as networks in this context, are mutually interrelated to the extent that a customer increase on one market triggers a certain reaction on a different market, indirectly increasing the utility for customers on the first market. However, the general problem of externalities is that actors might not take them into account correctly. This means that the decision of customers to join a market is not necessarily influenced by the positive externalities that are produced for other customers, possibly resulting in underincentive to join. Thus, platform intermediaries enabling different customer groups to interact in multi-sided markets might enhance efficiency from an economic welfare perspective.[17] The term "multi-sided" implies that the indirect network externalities and mutual interplay are not limited to two markets. These characteristics of multi-sided markets have implications for how these markets actually work, e.g. market mechanics like complex pricing. Pricing on multi-sided markets inter alia depends on the price elasticity of demand on every market mutually connected via (indirect) network externalities and the nature of these externalities. This means that even prices that are smaller than marginal costs on one side/market might be efficient to account for higher demand, thus ensuring higher indirect network effects on the other side/market.[18]

If these theoretical insights are transferred to the market for mobile operating systems, customers can be seen as part of different networks. In this example we

---

[14] *Rochet/Tirole*, Platform Competition in Two-Sided Markets, (2003) 1 Journal of the European Economic Association 990; *Evans*, The Antitrust Economics of Multi-Sided Platform Markets, (2003) 20 Yale Journal on Regulation 325; *Evans/Schmalensee*, Markets with Two-Sided Platforms, ISSUES IN COMPETITION LAW AND POLICY (ABA Section of Antitrust Law), Vol. 1, Chapter 28 (2008), available at: http://ssrn.com/abstract=1094820 (accessed 27 February 2014).

[15] Indirect network externalities describe the (indirect) increase of the utility of a user/user group by the increase in number of a different user group. Direct network externalities, in contrast, describe the effect that the utility of a user/user group increases if the number of the same user group grows (e.g. social networks, telecom networks) (*Evans*, *supra* note 14, at 332).

[16] *Evans*, *supra* note 14, at 331.

[17] *Evans*, *supra* note 14, at 332; *Rochet/Tirole*, *supra* note 14, at 991.

[18] *Evans/Schmalensee*, *supra* note 14, at 674.

shall distinguish between the network of smartphone manufacturers, MOS users and applications developers. In case the number of users of an MOS increases, this inter alia has an influence on the market for smartphone manufacturing and for the market of mobile applications. If more users are engaged in an MOS, it is more attractive for smartphone manufacturers to produce and support compatible devices (which indirectly increases user benefit) and it is more attractive for application developers to sell and support their products on the particular MOS (which also indirectly increases user benefit).[19] Thus, the market for mobile operating systems consists of competing user networks which are interrelated with other markets in a vertical structure through the existence of indirect network externalities. It should be mentioned that the interrelations of these different markets can also be seen from other perspectives, e.g. regarding the smartphone users as a distinct group or users of a certain application or application store.

The key insight is that for consumers it is not only relevant that they buy a smartphone which they like for whatever reason but that the installed operating system strongly influences their ability to adjust the device to their preferences by downloading applications or to profit from ongoing support. This however depends on the number of other persons who have that MOS installed on their device. For a competitor to enter the market for MOSs it is therefore essential to get multiple sides "on board" (including smartphone manufacturers and application developers) if they want to successfully compete.[20] Thus, it is not only the smartphone itself but rather the whole ecosystem surrounding it, specifically the MOS and applications/ services that can be accessed upon it, which have to be considered.[21] For consumers especially the availability of "top applications" they need in their daily life on an MOS can be more important than having access to a large number of applications that are compatible.[22] This can have consequences regarding the need to particularly have the providers of these "top applications" on board of an MOS, which could be problematic if these "must-have" applications belong to a different vertically integrated MOS provider (see Sect. 3.4 below).

---

[19] It should be remarked that there is no direct network effect, which means that an additional user of an MOS does not directly increase the benefit of other users of the same MOS.

[20] *Rochet/Tirole*, supra note 14, at 990.

[21] *Kenney/Pon*, supra note 8, at 241; Commission Decision, *Google/Motorola Mobility*, supra note 1, at para. 65. The Nemertes Research Group Inc. points out the importance of applications for the loss of market share of RIM's Blackberry OS to Apple's iOS and Google's Android, especially referring to the importance of a "rich app marketplace" and RIM's attempt to give incentives for application developers for their own OS. (The Nemertes Research Group Inc., RIM's 10k Offer Illustrates the Importance of Apps to Mobile Platform Adoption, 27 September 2012, available at: https://www.nemertes.com/reports/rim-s-10k-offer-illustrates-importance-apps-mobile-platform-adoption (accessed 27 February 2014)).

[22] *Dredge* refers to the launch of the MOS Blackberry 10 and the focus of the company on the availability of "top applications" on the MOS. *Dredge*, BlackBerry 10 launch shows the importance of top apps, Guardian News and Media Limited, 30 January 2013, available at: http://www.guardian.co.uk/technology/appsblog/2013/jan/30/blackberry-10-top-apps (accessed 27 February 2014).

From a competition policy perspective, the outlined market characteristics of MOSs result in three direct implications:

1) **Market-Entry Barriers**

   Potential competitors face high market-entry barriers, as they have to pull together several sides[23] (MOS user base, manufacturer base, application developer base/most-wanted applications[24]). However, this does not mean that it is impossible to enter a multi-sided market, because there is also a high incentive for potential competitors to become the dominant player in such a market in case superior solutions are offered.[25] Therefore, even being a dominant player on a multi-sided market, it is important to not fall behind alternative solutions. The question is rather whether the combination of different effects besides high market-entry barriers might deter potential entrants.

2) **Lock-in effects**

   Since MOS users indirectly profit from large networks and face significant switching costs (which can be strongly influenced by firms' strategies), they may be locked into an MOS depending on its characteristics. Moreover, customers can be locked in regarding their favorite applications.[26]

3) **Complex price design and complex competition policy assessment of firms' strategies**

   Since pricing is complex in multi-sided markets, the assessment of certain types of firms' behavior in the MOS market is difficult. Pricing that could be seen as predatory under certain circumstances might be just profit-maximizing in multi-sided markets.[27]

The next section addresses the question of competition concerns resulting from the above-mentioned characteristics of mobile communications markets. It will address inter- as well as intra-MOS competition.[28] In this respect, it is important to note that we assume that the majority of users do not conduct "multihoming" on different MOSs,[29] which would strongly influence competition parameters, because users would then use different smartphones with different MOSs, which is not the common type of conduct.

---

[23] *Rochet/Tirole*, *supra* note 14, at 990.

[24] Users are likely to not only care for smartphones themselves or the MOS usability, but for the ecosystem as a whole; "Do I have my favorite apps?".

[25] *Evans*, *supra* note 14, at 364.

[26] *Kenney/Pon*, *supra* note 8, at 242.

[27] *Evans/Schmalensee*, *supra* note 14, at 674.

[28] The observation of inter- or intra-platform competition can also refer to related fields such as technology platforms (*Distaso/Lupi/Manenti*, Platform Competition and Broadband Uptake: Theory and Empirical Evidence from the European Union (2005), at 2, available at: http://ideas.repec.org/p/wpa/wuwpio/0504019.html (accessed 27 February 2014)).

[29] *Rochet/Tirole*, *supra* note 14, at 991.

3 Competition Problems on the Market for Mobile Operating Systems

3.1 The Structure of Mobile Operating Systems and Competition Concerns

It is apparent that Google and Apple are the major players in the market for MOSs and at the same time are strongly vertically integrated. The question of whether these dominant players have the ability and incentive to vertically discriminate and distort (potential) competition depends on the assessment of market-entry barriers for potential competitors as well as lock-in effects (possibly influenced by firms' strategies).

Figure 1 shows the possibilities of vertical discrimination, tying and lock-in effects in a vertical structure with (dominant and vertically integrated) players in the MOS market. Thereby MOSs can run on multiple smartphone types (but are also inputs for smartphone manufacturers) and can host several types of application stores (application stores might also run on different MOSs). Moreover, applications can be offered by several application stores where one store offers a distinct number of applications.

In this illustration MOSs are seen as central in the sense of being inputs for smartphones[30] and the platform for application stores and applications.[31] Downstream discrimination refers to the potentially abusive behavior of dominant MOS providers to foreclose or otherwise discriminate against vendors of smartphones, application store providers or application developers that have or require access to the MOS. Downstream tying refers to the problem that MOS providers preinstall application stores and native applications on their MOS, where it is decisive whether the market for MOSs and the market for application stores and applications is really distinct.[32] Both tying and vertical discrimination are especially relevant in light of lock-in effects and high customer switching costs (in switching from one MOS to another), as this might increase the dominant firm's ability to discriminate (as a result of reduced competitive constraints), which might result in e.g. charging higher prices or types of foreclosure, and to

---

[30] Commission Decision, *Google/Motorola Mobility*, *supra* note 1, at para. 73.

[31] *Ibid.*, para. 22.

[32] *Au*, Anticompetitive Tying and Bundling Arrangements in the Smartphone Industry, (2012) 16 Stanford Technology Law Review 188, at 192. The concern about tying an MOS to a smartphone type should not be of much relevance if it is assumed that it is a precondition that a smartphone actually has an operating system when shipped to the consumer. Rather, the question whether smartphone manufacturers are locked into MOS providers can be of relevance and is discussed below (see Sect. 3.3).

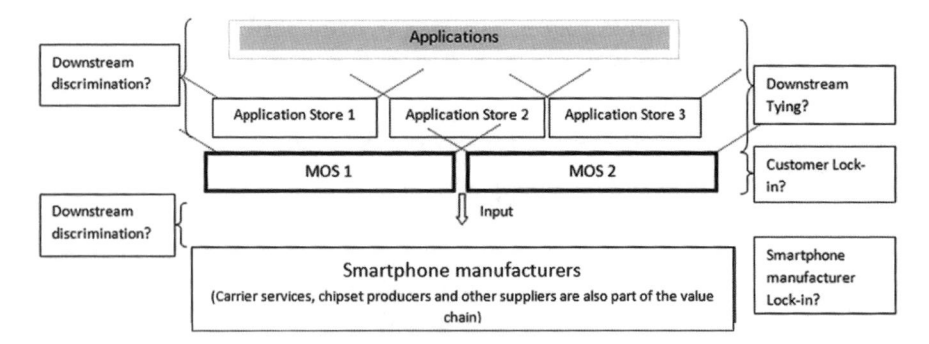

Fig. 1 Vertical discrimination in mobile communication (illustration by the author based on Commission Decision, *Google/Motorola Mobility, supra* note 1, at para. 22; *Kenney/Pon, supra* note 8, at 243, Fig. 2; *Au*, Anticompetitive Tying and Bundling Arrangements in the Smartphone Industry, (2012) 16 Stanford Technology Law Review 188, at 196)

leverage market power from the already dominant product to a different one through bundling or tying.[33]

In the following, three specific types of firms' conduct shall be further discussed: vertical discrimination, tying and the attempt to raise users' switching costs. In this respect, it is important to distinguish several competitive environments in which possibly abusive behavior can occur. As an example the following scenarios can be distinguished: if there exist only one MOS and one proprietary application store (hence, a monopolistic market), there is the risk that potential competitors might be foreclosed and therefore a disciplinary constraint on firms' behavior by potential competition might be impeded. In a scenario where there is one MOS but several application stores (which means that proprietary and non-proprietary application stores compete) there is the incentive of the MOS-provider to discriminate downstream. Finally, in a scenario with different MOSs competing with each other and different application stores available on these different MOSs, high switching costs of users can be the reason why e.g. a user might not switch to a different MOS (which better suits the user's preferences) or the MOS provider might charge higher prices in a proprietary application store.[34] Therefore, the types of conduct that are relevant depend on the competitive situation and can be related to actual or potential competition.

---

[33] *Kenney/Pon, supra* note 8, at 240.

[34] *Au, supra* note 32, at 196.

3.2 Vertical Discrimination on Mobile Operating Systems

Vertical discrimination is possible on MOSs or in application stores by price design, which means charging discriminatory high prices for the use of an MOS (e.g. license fees) or discriminatory fees for the use of an application store (e.g. royalties based on turnover shares). The same result can be produced by discriminatory low prices for a (vertically integrated) MOS provider's own products (e.g. a specific proprietary application which is offered free of charge in an MOS provider's own application store due to cross-subsidization from other business areas of the dominant MOS provider). However, it is important to note that discriminatory low prices are hard to assess in multi-sided markets since for such a judgment the indirect network externalities and other characteristics of the multi-sided market have to be considered. If on one market discriminatory low prices are suspected, this does not necessarily allow the conclusion that this is in fact abusive since the low price might legitimately account for the creation of a higher user base and an increase in indirect network externalities, thus entailing additional consumer benefits.[35] A second way to discriminate vertically is by foreclosing competitors (e.g. by restricting access to an MOS or an application store or by offering minor integration or support).[36] In the past antitrust concerns were raised both in the EU and the US with regard to the behavior of Google of potentially displaying biased web search results favoring its own services. However, in the US the evidence collected was not such as to conclude an antitrust violation,[37] while in the EU the Commission seeks to secure binding commitments by Google to clear competition concerns.[38] Similarly to this type of conduct, vertical discrimination could also be a theoretical threat to competition in proprietary MOS application stores. If downstream products of the vertically integrated MOS provider are preferred in the general search results of proprietary application stores, competitors' products are consequently harder to find.

---

[35] *Evans, supra* note 14, at 367.

[36] It should be mentioned that charging discriminatory high prices is also a form of foreclosing competitors.

[37] FTC (Federal Trade Commission): Google Agrees to Change Its Business Practices to Resolve FTC Competition Concerns In the Markets for Devices Like Smart Phones, Games and Tablets, and in Online Search, 3 January 2013, available at: http://ftc.gov/opa/2013/01/google.shtm (accessed 27 February 2014).

[38] Almunia, Joaquín (Vice President of the European Commission responsible for Competition Policy) (2012): Statement by Vice President Almunia on the Google investigation, (SPEECH/12/967, 18 December 2012).

3.3 Tying in the Sphere of Mobile Operating Systems

Tying refers to a firm's conduct by which products that can be sold separately are sold together to leverage market power from one product (where the firm was dominant previously) to a different product.[39] Transferred to MOS this means that a dominant firm in this market may e.g. preinstall an application on the MOS to gain market power regarding this product as well (this however is strongly influenced by switching costs or lock-in effects of users relating to the applications involved).

As a direct comparison, the case in which Microsoft was accused of tying its "Internet Explorer" to the operating system "Windows" may be mentioned.[40] The argument of competition authorities both in the US and the EU was that operating systems and browsers were separate markets while Microsoft had a dominant position in the market for PC operating systems.[41] Moreover, it was not possible for Windows users (before Windows 7) to obtain the operating system without the Internet Explorer or to de-install the software.[42] Thus, market power on the market for PC operating systems was leveraged to the browser market, where competition was impeded. The European Commission settled the case with Microsoft on the basis of commitments by Microsoft to give users the ability to turn the Internet Explorer on or off, to enable them to install a different browser and to present a choice screen to customers allowing for a free choice of several competing web browsers.[43]

Similarly, remedies were imposed in the US that aimed at enabling more competition on the web browser market.[44] This example illustrates to what extent a prominent tying case from a different sector shows similarities to competition concerns on the MOS market and could be transferred to a scenario where an MOS provider preinstalls applications (e.g. a mobile internet browser) with the possible aim to leverage market power. However, three crucial preconditions for an abusive

---

[39] *Au, supra* note 32, at 197.

[40] United States v Microsoft, 253 F.3d 34 (2001); Commission Decision of 16 December 2009 relating to a proceeding under Article 102 of the Treaty on the Functioning of the European Union and Article 54 of the EEA Agreement (Case COMP/C-3/39.530 – *Microsoft* (tying)), see also *Kenney/Pon, supra* note 8, at 240.

[41] United States v Microsoft, 253 F.3d 34 (2001), at 41, 54; Commission Decision, *Microsoft* (tying), *supra* note 40, at paras 17, 24, 30.

[42] Commission Decision, *Microsoft* (tying), *supra* note 40, at para. 36.

[43] *Ibid.* Annex: The Commitments, at paras 1, 7–17. In 2013 the European Commission imposed a fine of €561 million on Microsoft for not complying with the settlement commitments (Commission Decision of 6 March 2013 addressed to Microsoft Corporation relating to a proceeding on the imposition of a fine pursuant to Article 23(2)(c) of Council Regulation (EC) No 1/2003 for failure to comply with a commitment made binding by a Commission decision pursuant to Article 9 of Council Regulation (EC) No 1/2003, Case AT.39530 (Microsoft - Tying), Article 1 and Article 2).

[44] United States v Microsoft, 231 F.Supp.2d 144 (2002); see also *Au, supra* note 32, at 202.

tying arrangement are, in analogy to the *Microsoft* case, that the firm is dominant in the MOS market (which yet is not necessarily the case concerning Apple's iOS and Google's Android since it is rather a duopoly market), that the dominant MOS provider does not enable consumers to buy and run the MOS and the tied product separately from each other and that MOS and on-top applications are really distinct markets.[45]

The question whether MOS and application stores are distinct markets can probably not be answered in affirmative if the MOS is seen as the basis for build-upon applications and users see the application store as a necessary and inherent feature to access (third-party and proprietary) applications conveniently. On the other hand, it can be argued that MOSs themselves are programs that compete on the basis of their usability and can be licensed to different manufacturers and run on a variety of mobile devices. The important factor for users should rather be the ability to download applications to the MOS, not the default availability of a specific application store. Moreover, application stores can compete on the basis of usability, payment methods and price. Therefore, argued from this perspective, the limitation to only one application store on one MOS would reduce consumer benefits and foreclose potential competition through different application stores.[46]

This shows the difficulties to determine potentially abusive tying arrangements in the MOS market, as it is not clear, even if real dominance of one MOS provider occurs, whether there exists a distinct consumer demand for elements of an MOS (in the sense that there exists a consumer demand for the tied product and the tying product separately) or whether these elements can be seen as inherent features of the MOS.[47] Currently, both Apple and Google in their respective MOSs install a variety of applications on their devices (including the application stores "App Store" and "Play Store", respectively). Some of these applications seem to be deeply integrated in the MOS and not easy to de-install from the device. Moreover, the use of some types of applications or services requires connections to other (complementary) services, which means that the de-installation or shut-down of one could impede the other.[48]

---

[45] *Au, supra* note 32, at 203.
[46] *Ibid.*, at 207.
[47] *Ibid.*
[48] E.g. it is a precondition to have a Google (Email) account (Gmail) to be able to download applications from the Google Play application store.

3.4 Switching Costs on Mobile Operating Systems

There exist several possible strategies for firms to raise users' switching costs on mobile operating systems. It should be kept in mind that this influences market-entry barriers and abilities of firms to vertically discriminate including foreclosure strategies. Generally, it can be observed that vertically integrated MOS providers like Apple and Google offer diverse complementary and connected services which raise user's costs of switching to a different MOS. An example of this is the cloud-based[49] synchronization of contacts and calendar data or installed applications and downloaded media like music or books. If a new MOS is chosen by the user, it is not entirely clear whether synchronization of data will work on the new system or whether it has to be set up again. A related question is whether content (like applications or media files) that users have bought for use on the former MOS can be used on the new MOS. Following this line of argument, a user is more likely to stick to the former MOS when a decision on a new handset is to be made, because this ensures data synchronization and other complementarities referring to the former handset. If there is a risk that content already paid for cannot be used on the new MOS, this incurs significant switching costs. Moreover, it is questionable if a user's favorite applications will run, or will even be available, on a new MOS—a question that typically does not arise if the user retains his current MOS which is perhaps run on a different device.[50] Additional costs are caused by switching to a different MOS, since users are likely to be required to set up their settings anew, and possibly different user accounts. Part of these set-up costs can raise concerns regarding privacy and data protection, since it might be a problem for users to submit their data to different companies (though it could also be a problem to submit too much data to one company). It should be kept in mind in this context that complementary services within one MOS offer users additional benefits when they use this system. For example, if users are offered complementary services by vertically integrated MOS providers, they can typically use one user account for multiple services, a situation that should be more convenient and also reduces the amount of data revealed to different companies. However, if the user is tied or locked into an MOS so that a better mobile device or better MOS is still not preferred over the incumbent, this is problematic for potential or actual competitors. A look at the current characteristics of the two most successful MOSs, Android and iOS, shows many signs of complementarities within the MOS but also high user switching costs or even lock-in effects.[51]

---

[49] The term "cloud services" refers to the provision of services through the internet (e.g. storage, synchronization or processing of data) (*Armbrust/Fox/Griffith/Joseph/Katz/Konwinski/Lee/Patterson/Rabkin/Stoica/Zaharia*, Above the Clouds: A Berkeley View of Cloud Computing, Technical Report No. UCB/EECS-2009-28, (2009), at 4, available at: http://www.eecs.berkeley.edu/Pubs/TechRpts/2009/EECS-2009-28.html (accessed 27 February 2014)).

[50] Commission Decision, *Google/Motorola Mobility*, supra note 1, at para. 25.

[51] *Kenney/Pon*, supra note 8, at 242.

It should be mentioned that manufacturers of smartphones also face switching costs if they decide to ship their devices with a different MOS installed. From a customer perspective, it is important that their favored applications are available on the new MOS (especially the must-have applications). If this is not the case, there is a high risk of users not accepting the smartphone manufacturer's switch to the new MOS. Thus, a decision of a smartphone manufacturer to vertically integrate and develop its own MOS might be deterred if important applications are not compatible. Keeping in mind that Apple and Google are suppliers of diverse applications (which are possibly must-have applications[52]), it is questionable whether they would adapt their applications to a new competitor in the MOS market. Recently, there have been complaints by Microsoft in the course of bringing its MOS Windows Phone to the market that there is no adequate application to access Google's video sharing platform YouTube that features the same user experience as on Android devices. However, it is generally doubtful whether application developers—particularly if they are vertically integrated like Google or Apple—have to supply their applications to rival MOSs if the argument can be made that it is not worthwhile to develop applications for a new MOS with a relatively small market share. A related question is whether the application, if it is also made available for the new MOS, has to offer the same user experience and whether it can raise competition concerns if this is not the case. Google in the mentioned case denied Microsoft's allegation, referring to the possibility for Windows Phone users to access the YouTube service.[53] This example shows that the vertical integration of MOS providers can be problematic if their applications are a must-have for consumers (which however may be difficult to define), and therefore might deter the smartphone manufacturers from developing their own MOSs or switching to different ones.[54] Although for smartphone manufacturers the Google Android MOS is free of charge, they are dependent on Google in the sense that every device shipped with the Android MOS and preinstalled Google applications has to be approved by Google concerning the MOS and the preinstalled Google applications.[55]

3.5 Competition Through Countervailing Factors on Mobile Operating Systems

There exists one important countervailing factor in particular in assessing the ability of MOS providers to vertically discriminate in the form of e.g. foreclosure

---

[52] Examples could be Google's YouTube App, Google Maps or Apple's iTunes App.

[53] *Gannes*, Microsoft: Google Is (Still) Blocking Us From Building YouTube for Windows Phone, 2 January 2013, available at: http://allthingsd.com/20130102/microsoft-google-is-still-blocking-us-from-building-youtube-for-windows-phone/ (accessed 27 February 2014).

[54] Commission Decision, *Google/Motorola Mobility*, *supra* note 1, at para. 25.

[55] *Ibid.*, at paras 66, 67.

of competitors, tying or charging high prices. The built-in mobile internet browser on MOS can be seen as an access point for applications but also application stores. Therefore, a limitation to a preinstalled version of an application store or restrictions concerning provided applications can be circumvented by users when a download via built-in mobile internet browsers is possible.[56] This becomes evident in the case of Google's Android MOS, in which there exists the possibility to download the Amazon App Store via the mobile internet browser. The Amazon App Store offers diverse applications also available in the Google Play Store but provides different prices and different payment methods (i.e. by EC card),[57] thus leading to intra-platform competition. Therefore, this solution can be seen as "competitive relief"[58] for a lack of the possibility to choose multiple application stores in contrast to a preinstalled one. However, in comparison to downloading applications via the built-in application store, the download through a mobile internet browser is more complicated, inconvenient and lengthy due to the fact that different applications have to be accessed through different web pages. Moreover, downloads or updates are not necessarily synchronized via cloud services, which is important if users switch to a different smartphone with the same MOS. Besides the direct download and installation of applications through the mobile internet browser, the set-up of a new application store (like the Amazon app store) also entails considerable costs. Currently, the installation of the Amazon App Store for Android is only possible by following a certain procedure that is explained by Amazon on its homepage. This includes the manual change of settings concerning the installation of "unknown files" from a mobile internet browser.[59] Assessing whether competitive relief in the form of additional access points for buying applications leads to e.g. price competition and innovation in payment methods is therefore a question of consumers' switching costs and relative costs that go along with the use of these new access points.[60] In order to calculate the effectiveness of such competitive relief, it is important to know how many cross-platform applications are available, because this determines the possibility of accessing such applications without the dependence on a specific MOS or application store.[61]

---

[56] *Au, supra* note 32, at 224. The question whether a preinstalled built-in mobile internet browser is a competition concern is discussed above in Sect. 3.3.

[57] *Au, supra* note 32, at 221.

[58] *Ibid.*, at 224.

[59] Amazon.com, Inc., Getting Started with the Amazon Appstore - Install the Amazon Appstore, available at: https://www.amazon.com/gp/feature.html?ie=UTF8&docId=1000626391&ref_=amb_link_363093842_2 (accessed 27 February 2014).

[60] *Au, supra* note 32, at 226.

[61] *Ibid.*, at 224.

4 Competition Law and Markets for Mobile Operating Systems

The previous section outlined potential competition concerns from a rather theoretical perspective based on current MOS characteristics. Since there exist potential threats for competition and innovation arising from the structure of the MOS market, it is relevant to think about possible ways for competition policy to mitigate actual or upcoming competition concerns and to keep markets contestable.

In the EU, Article 102 TFEU, referring to an abuse of a dominant position in the internal market, is applicable only when undertakings are dominant. This is currently not necessarily the case in the MOS market since two major players dominate. Thus, the situation of Google and Apple cannot be directly transferred to the *Microsoft* case, where one company clearly dominated the market for PC operating systems. Because there have not actually been any antitrust cases regarding the MOS market, it is not clear whether Article 102 TFEU would be applicable or not. However, if the market conditions change, this question might be answered differently. Although there might occur types of conduct on the MOS market that show parallels to cases which have been deemed anticompetitive by competition authorities and courts in the past, the question of the correct market delineation e.g. in terms of whether a certain application store or an application is an MOS feature or a distinct market is still unclear,[62] as is the question of how the related markets for (mobile) advertising are connected herewith.[63]

In order to derive some basic insight from actual competition cases, reference can be made to a vertical merger that took place in 2012 between Google, the provider of the MOS Android, and Motorola Mobility, a manufacturer of mobile handsets, and the competitive assessment of this merger in the EU. The merger was cleared in the EU subject to certain commitments by Google concerning standard-essential patents owned by Motorola Mobility.[64] In its analysis the European Commission for the first time defined a relevant product market for MOSs for smartphones and tablet devices as distinct from the MOSs for basic mobile phones or PC operating systems.[65] Regarding the question of Google's market share in the MOS market, the Commission noted that based on a market investigation it was evident that Google controlled the Android MOS ecosystem while every device running Android should account for Google's market share in the MOS market (which at that time was 40–50 % in the European Economic Area).[66] The Commission consequently assessed the question whether Google, as vertically integrated due to the merger, would have the ability and incentive to vertically

---

[62] *Au, supra* note 32, at 206.
[63] E.g. Commission Decision, *Google/Motorola Mobility, supra* note 1, at paras 87, 88.
[64] Commission Decision, *Google/Motorola Mobility, supra* note 1, at paras 9, 181, 182.
[65] *Ibid.,* at para. 29.
[66] *Ibid.,* at paras 64–72.

discriminate. Specifically, the Commission addressed the questions of whether a vertically integrated Google-Motorola Mobility had the ability to foreclose inputs (meaning the Android MOS), the incentive to do so and whether this would impede effective competition on downstream markets i.e. concerning smartphone manufacturers' access to Android.[67] In analyzing Google's ability to vertically discriminate, the Commission pointed out that, as supplier of Android, Google could impede competition with other smartphone manufacturers by favoring Motorola Mobility in terms of the integration of the MOS. Moreover, Google had the ability to discriminate by the use of approval proceedings for devices that ran with Android and proprietary applications used by competitors (also referring to competitors' business information potentially being transferred to Motorola Mobility). Google also had the ability to offer inferior support for competing Android devices (e.g. in terms of a discriminatory update policy for Android run on competitors' devices).[68] However, the Commission noted that the merger with Motorola Mobility did not increase Google's ability to discriminate vertically since the possibilities to do so existed before the merger and independently of Motorola Mobility.[69]

In assessing Google's incentive to vertically discriminate, the Commission paid special attention to the core business of Google concerning the MOS and related services, which was mobile advertising.[70] The Commission referred to a market investigation indicating that for Google other smartphone manufacturers played a bigger role regarding mobile advertising revenues than Motorola Mobility did, which rendered it unlikely that Google would favor Motorola Mobility regarding the Android MOS. Considering the increasing importance of mobile revenues for Google in contrast to the low hardware margins stemming from Motorola Mobility, the Commission held it very unlikely that Google would eventually favor Motorola Mobility and would risk having other smartphone manufacturers switch to rival MOS providers.[71] Therefore, the Commission concluded that a combined Google-Motorola Mobility had the ability to vertically discriminate to restrict competitors' access to the Android MOS (which was already present before the merger), but that it did not have the incentive to do so.[72] Although Android was regarded as an important input for smartphone manufacturers, the Commission added that in case of unilaterally restricted access or downgraded quality of the Android MOS, most competitors could circumvent discriminatory conduct by using a competing MOS or in some cases develop their own MOS. Moreover, those smartphone manufacturers who were affected by such conduct would be rather small in comparison to

---

[67] *Ibid.*, at para. 79; The European Commission is citing the "Guidelines on the assessment of non-horizontal mergers under the Council Regulation on the control of concentrations between undertakings", [2008] OJ C 265/6, para. 32.

[68] Commission Decision, *Google/Motorola Mobility*, *supra* note 1, at para 81.

[69] *Ibid.*, at para. 85.

[70] *Ibid.*, at paras 87–93.

[71] *Ibid.*, at paras 86–94.

[72] *Ibid.*, at paras 85, 94.

other competitors that have their own proprietary MOSs (like Apple or Blackberry) or use more than one MOS for their devices. This was said to imply that even if discriminatory conduct did take place, it would not have much relevance for effective competition.[73] In assessing whether Motorola Mobility would have the incentive to restrict access to their smartphones for other MOS developers post-merger, the Commission stated that previously Motorola Mobility used Android exclusively on their devices, so that a merger with Google would not change the competitive situation. Since the market share of Motorola Mobility was rather minor, there were sufficient competing smartphone manufacturers as potential buyers of MOSs (especially keeping in mind that some of them used more than one MOS for their devices), which implied that discriminatory conduct in this sense would not have much of an influence on effective competition.[74] Hence, it could be summarized that vertical discrimination regarding the Android MOS and Motorola Mobility in the described ways was theoretically possible but either unlikely to occur or not likely to have much influence on competition between MOS providers and smartphone manufacturers.[75]

Parallel to the investigations in the EU, the US Department of Justice (US DOJ) similarly cleared the Google-Motorola Mobility merger after mainly focusing on the question of whether there was ability and incentive for the merging parties to discriminate on the basis of intellectual property rights. This was especially important against the background of Google acquiring approximately 17,000 issued patents and 6,800 patent applications in the course of the transaction (among which were hundreds of standard-essential patents, i.e. those essential for the implementation of the respective standard in producing mobile devices).[76] The US DOJ argued that the change of ownership of Motorola Mobility and its patents was not likely to change the competitive environment, based in part on public statements by the parties. Although the merger might have caused potential benefits for the parties to raise rivals' costs by exploiting the newly acquired patent base, the DOJ made clear that this was not likely to change the already existing types of

---

[73] *Ibid.*, at paras 95–99.

[74] *Ibid.*, at paras 100–103.

[75] The Commission in the merger case *Google/Motorola Mobility* also looked at discriminatory conduct regarding standard-essential patents and commitments to charge fair, reasonable and non-discriminatory license fees (FRAND commitments) and assessed the resulting abilities and incentives of Google-Motorola Mobility post-merger. It concluded that the IPR-based discriminatory potential was limited (Commission Decision, *Google/Motorola Mobility*, *supra* note 1, at paras 109–160).

[76] US DOJ (Department of Justice): Statement of the Department of Justice's Antitrust Division on Its Decision to Close Its Investigations of Google Inc.'s Acquisition of Motorola Mobility Holdings Inc. and the Acquisitions of Certain Patents by Apple Inc., Microsoft Corp. and Research in Motion Ltd., 13 February 2012, available at: http://www.justice.gov/opa/pr/2012/February/12-at-210.html (accessed 27 February 2014).

conduct of the parties.[77] In the EU, the assessment of a potential impediment to effective competition relating to the use of intellectual property rights (i.e. standard-essential patents) also played an important role in the assessment of the Google-Motorola Mobility merger.[78]

The merger case *Google/Motorola Mobility* points to two important insights: First, there is a relevant market regarding MOSs as distinct and smartphone-based, and the MOS is "a central part of a smart mobile device".[79] Second, competition concerns due to vertical integration on the MOS market like foreclosure strategies and tying refer to types of conduct that are not new and can be transferred to the MOS market taking into account abilities and incentives for anticompetitive behavior.[80] Keeping in mind that a case regarding MOS markets would probably be brought forward under Art. 102 TFEU, it is clear that the criterion of market dominance has to be considered besides the assessment of specific types of conduct. Countervailing efficiency advantages, e.g. with regard to the bundling of MOS with complementary applications, are also significant assessment criteria since users profit directly if they can use well-integrated and well-connected applications on an MOS.[81] Accordingly, there are costs involved in alternative and possibly more inconvenient solutions. For example, it would be possible to present a choice screen that appears after installation of an MOS, though this would require much more time and set-up costs, compared to a scenario where relevant services are preinstalled by the MOS provider.

5 Conclusion

As the importance of mobile communications increases, it is evident that two mobile operating systems are dominating the market and are deeply vertically integrated. Markets for mobile operating systems are multi-sided markets with indirect network externalities. Competition concerns with the MOS market can arise in fields concerning market-entry barriers, consumer switching costs/lock-in, vertical discrimination (e.g. tying, foreclosure) and related conduct. Types of conduct on the MOS market might occur which show patterns that resemble practices which raised competition concerns in the past. It becomes obvious that the correct market delineation, especially regarding integrated application stores and applications, is rather difficult in this context. It is likely that the instruments available in competition law are sufficient to address the concerns regarding the MOS market. However, they should be applied carefully due to the complexity of

---

[77] *Ibid.*

[78] Commission Decision, *Google/Motorola Mobility, supra* note 1, at paras 109–160.

[79] *Ibid.*, at para. 24.

[80] *Ibid.*, at para. 77.

[81] *Au, supra* note 32, at 226.

the MOS market, and accordingly adjusted to its characteristics. This is especially true since business models of the relevant players rely heavily on the connection of user data and its monetization through advertising and not necessarily through the sale of products to the user. This means that certain types of conduct might turn out to be problematic if the specific importance of data and ecosystems are taken into account. The concerns discussed in this note might eventually turn out to be more significant in the future, depending on the development of market shares of relevant players and firms' strategies. Therefore, in ensuring the prospective contestability of MOS markets, the role of competition policy might be to set clear boundaries regarding anticompetitive conduct in mobile communications by the use of the existing competition rules.

Acknowledgment I thank Prof. Dr. Wolfgang Kerber and my colleague Dipl. Volksw. Julia Wendel for helpful comments. The author is of course responsible for all remaining errors.

The More Technological Approach: Competition Law in the Digital Economy

Rupprecht Podszun

The claim that the internet has changed everything is a commonplace in blogs and presentations. It is definitely untrue, though, for competition law. If one compares the rules and the application of the rules in Europe in 2014 and in 1994 it is hard to spot a principal difference that is causally linked to the rise of the internet—apart from the facts of some cases: nowadays, mobile phones are more important than landlines, media houses fight for advertising budget in the net, and big brands force their distributors to polish their virtual stores instead of brick-and-mortar-stores. So, mainstream competition law has it that a website essentially is nothing but a high-street shop.

Nothing has changed. Legislators have refrained from changing competition law rules for the digital age. European lawmakers took the constituencies by surprise when they decided not to address the internet in the 2010 block exemption regulation on vertical restraints. It is only in the accompanying Guidelines that the internet has a role (as Stefan Enchelmaier points out in his contribution). Ever since, academics and practitioners have tried to press online experiences into an offline-world wording. The application of competition law to internet cases involving Google and the like has likewise not seen revolutionary changes, or so it seems. When another conference on competition law and internet was announced a scholar in the field recently told me: "What is all the fuss about? You just apply the rules, and that's it!"

Business as usual? A new sector with some new factual features that require special attention, but nothing revolutionary? I beg to differ. Digitalization has changed the economy as a whole. Processes are reorganized in companies, new products emerge, old players stumble and digital natives have a competitive edge. Probably, the emergence of the internet and the progress of information technology are comparable only to game-changing events like the invention of electricity or

---

R. Podszun (✉)
University of Bayreuth, Bayreuth, Germany, and Max Planck Institute for Innovation and Competition, Munich, Germany
e-mail: LS-podszun@uni-bayreuth.de

letterpress printing (while the internet combines both, in a way). Of course, the changes affect different industries with different speed and with different intensity. Yet, my humble experience tells me that there is not a single forward-thinking undertaking that is not influenced heavily by digitalization.

In my view, such revolutionary events in economics must leave their mark on the rules that we consider the basic rules of the market economy.[1] The essays collected in this book on competition on the internet give an idea of what we could talk about when taking the challenge of adopting rules for the digital age. Two questions spring to my mind, and I will try to answer with a view to the contributions in this volume: Firstly, what characterizes the digitalized economy? Are there significant changes to doing business? If this is the case, it makes sense to reconsider the rules of competition law. Secondly, do these changes prompt a conceptual reconsideration of competition law? Or is it possible to accommodate concerns within the traditional conceptual framework? Under this heading I will discuss whether new competition law paradigms are necessary. In my conclusion, I suggest a "more technological approach".

Apart from digitalization other trends have influenced competition law in the past years: the international proliferation of competition law regimes, the rise of private enforcement, and the new possibilities of economics, for instance. I acknowledge that these agents of change have had an enormous impact as well and are interconnected with the internet.

1 Characteristics of the Digital Economy

The term "digital economy" was coined by Don Tapscott as early as 1995, when he projected the changes for businesses due to the increasing influence of the internet.[2] Tapscott identified 12 "themes of the new economy": knowledge, digitization, virtualization, molecularization, integration, disintermediation, convergence, innovation, prosumption, immediacy, globalization and discordance.[3] The thesis of the early apostles of the digital economy was that these themes not only seize internet firms or media companies that are directly connected with information and communication technologies (ICT), but they even change the economy as a whole. Now, a decade and a half later, no manager would deny and no economic regulator could ignore the impact of the internet on doing business. Actually, these "themes" have hit hard on traditional undertakings, new players emerged and the external distribution structure changed as much as internal organization and communication

---

[1] I think this is also true for the significant change we saw from an economy dominated by industry to an economy dominated by finance, cf. *Fikentscher/Hacker/Podszun*, FairEconomy (2013), pp. 49 ff.

[2] *Tapscott*, Die digitale Revolution, 1996.

[3] *Tapscott*, Die digitale Revolution, 1996, pp. 64 ff.

processes. The cases discussed in this book deliver a rich panorama of "new facts". Reviewing these, I would go even further than Simonetta Vezzoso, who begins her chapter with a characterization of the internet as a basic economic infrastructure and an additional market space—in my view our economy has undergone an even more fundamental change. To demonstrate this, I refer to the 12 topics Don Tapscott identified as characteristic for the digital economy. Taking all the developments together shows that this is not merely an additional feature of the economy, but something new.

- Knowledge: The economy is knowledge-driven, products contain more specific information and the value of a company is dependent upon its knowledge. The whole business model of Google, presented in this book by Ronny Hauck, is based on superior information, and thus on knowledge. Sebastian Wismer, writing on price parity clauses, presents a mechanism to deal with information deficits. Pablo Ibàñez Colomo's contribution on the fight for access (as for instance in the *Microsoft* case) deals in great measure with access to knowledge.
- Digitization: The information is digitized and therefore has a medium that is easily transferrable at high speed and low cost. This is a completely different raw material than steel or coal. Think of the eBooks that form the object of analysis of Simonetta Vezzoso, or the digitized information searched and (allegedly) "scraped" by Google.
- Virtualization: Goods and shops and meetings and money exist in a virtual dimension, i.e. without a tangible materialization in the "real world". Virtual worlds exist on handhelds nowadays, as Simonetta Vezzoso and Jonas Severin Frank point out. Stefan Enchelmaier makes it clear when dealing with selective distribution in the light of the Pierre Fabre judgment that nowadays selective distribution means having a website plus an automated warehouse on the motorway instead of a luxury shop in the pedestrian zone.
- Molecularization: Undertakings can be split into ever smaller business units. They can interact in a far more direct way with customers. The tendency of having centralized giants is overcome. While companies may still be large, the links within the company are often less strict and customer relations are much more focused. Close links between companies and customers play a more important role than before for some of the undertakings covered in this volume, eBook-publishers for instance, or Amazon, HRS or the mobile phone industry.
- Integration: The internet is a network and the whole idea is to bring people and companies closer together. This leads to networking structures and to new combinations of technologies, knowledge, investment or ideas that in former times did not have fora for interaction. A forum that is in the focus of competition law is platforms, a recurring topic in this book. Network effects in multi-sided markets are the result.
- Disintermediation: One of the most visible structural changes is that intermediaries such as distributors may lose their business. Due to the possibility to address customers directly and process their data, some businesses no longer need the work of some middle-men. Nearly all contributions deal with this

extinction or reform of the distribution channels. Simonetta Vezzoso presents the new agency models in eBook sales that have replaced traditional wholesale models. The background to Stefan Enchelmaier's part is the wish of producers to control their distribution channels and to stop internet sales. Pablo Ibàñez Colomo dedicates his contribution to vertical integration and possible strategies of discrimination against others. He names *Google* or *Microsoft* but also the post-merger scenario for the *Microsoft/Skype* case. Amazon and HRS, the topic of Sebastian Wismer's chapter, are integrating vertically, as are Google (Ronny Hauck) and the mobile phone companies like Google and Apple (Jonas Severin Frank).

- Convergence: The convergence of computer technology, the communication industry and content providers has led to a new form of economic power that bundles these three sectors. The undertakings that combine the three forces dominate and drive the markets. Typical examples in the mobile markets include Apple and Google, as shown by Frank. The same convergence happened in the eBooks-market, where Apple and Amazon fought for market leadership in all segments.
- Innovation: Innovation and creativity play a much larger role today, since the life cycle of products, ideas and firms has decreased. New technologies have enabled waves of innovation. Since any innovative step enables new research and development, it is in the nature of innovation to keep spiraling. Mobile internet is an example of this tendency. The whole ICT sector is of course driven by innovation, and it is not just products, but also business models that are innovative and new—see Google for instance.
- Prosumption: This artificial term characterizes the role of consumers in production. Consumers and users are involved in product design or give individual feedback. A typical example is user-generated content that is an element of commercial business models while generated by consumers who also pay for the good or service thus created. Consumers also contribute heavily to network effects by passing on their information, thereby keeping production costs low for the producers.
- Immediacy: Due to the speed of information transmittal and the possibility to process data automatically, the immediacy of business events has grown. Everything happens much faster than before and thus changes the strategies of companies. Stefan Enchelmaier gives examples of this, such as when customers start to check prices online while shopping.
- Globalization: Of course, the phenomenon of globalization has many roots, but it is definitely influenced in part by internet technologies that enable communication and the proliferation of business models or products. Internationalization is an aspect of every undertaking's strategy since markets have been opened up everywhere—with the support of internet technologies. Customers can easily find sources of goods in other countries over the internet. Parallel trade, as in the example Stefan Enchelmaier includes, is a typical example of this.
- Discordance: Finally, all these themes seen together form a new fundament for the economy. It is no longer just an economy that is a bit faster or a bit more

global or a bit more interconnected than before. While every single aspect may be not-so-revolutionary, the combination and the dimension of these single aspects add up to a very significant change: The economy is a digital one, characterized by fast speed, dependence upon technology, new business models, closer ties, less costs and a global playing field. Such a shift means that the traditional distribution of wealth, resources and chances is shattered. Privileges and benefits are under attack, access—as Pablo Ibàñez Colomo points out—becomes vital. Tapscott, accordingly, sees discordance, social clashes, as inevitable. Courts and enforcement agencies have difficulties in handling the new developments and some of the scholars in this volume have detected inconsistency in the jurisprudence. Maybe this unpredictability is not a sign of judicial fallibility but of the discordance in the economy making itself felt in law-making.

When the European Commission proposed a Digital Agenda for Europe in 2010, it assumed that 5 % of the European GDP is directly attributable to the ICT sector.[4] Yet, the Commission also pointed out that the importance of the sector is by far greater than this number indicates, due to its dynamics and innovative power. The Commission also highlighted the social role of internet networks changing the lifestyles of European consumers, workers and bosses alike. And, verbatim: "The development of high-speed networks today is having the same revolutionary impact as the development of electricity and transportation networks had a century ago."[5] The small review of the "classic" definition of a digital economy undertaken above shows that the characteristics of such an economy are well-established aspects of today's business life—as is proved by the cases that the authors of this volume discuss.

2 Conceptual Issues for Competition Law

If even the European Commission confirms that an economy is undergoing a revolution, can lawyers stand by and watch what happens? Or is it their task to review the essential body of economic law? An economy dominated by new driving forces needs a competition law that is adapted to these new forces.

The underlying assumption of the analyses in this book is that the rules in place are generally well-crafted to deal with the matters of the digital economy. The prohibition of restrictive business agreements and of the abuse of market dominance as well as merger control are established, and most general rules seem to be broad enough to be interpreted in meaningful ways. The flexibility of the general clauses allows enforcers to tackle a traditional cement cartel as well as a merger

---

[4] Communication from the Commission, A Digital Agenda for Europe, 19 May 2010 COM(2010) 245 final, at 4.
[5] Communication from the Commission, A Digital Agenda for Europe, 19 May 2010 COM(2010) 245 final, at 4.

between Microsoft and Skype or a licensing problem in telecommunications technology. Accompanying legislation such as the block exemption regulations or the guidelines handed down by the European Commission seems more apt for reform. The application of the rules in specific cases will be the main battleground for modern concepts of competition law. The authors of the papers have shown this in the individual circumstances.

In all cases, though, the difficulties in coming to terms with the internet phenomena were palpable. Fresh ideas are needed, and maybe even more: a shift of paradigms. In the texts in this book, I identify three recurring features: the translation issue, the economics issue and the enforcement issue.

By translation I mean the difficulty of practitioners and scholars to translate digital or virtual phenomena into a language of the past. Stefan Enchelmaier's description of "selective distribution" via websites on the one hand and high-street shops on the other and his comments on the Commission's quest for "equivalent criteria" is the most compelling example. Yet, other terms of competition law need new interpretations as well. Ronny Hauck for instance asks what the "market entry barriers" are for competitors to the Google Search engine. User data could help Google to foreclose the market—a virtual currency yet to be integrated in the canon of symptoms for dominance. The legal terminology, framed in the 1950s, in an age of coal and steel, struggles with virtual, digital goods and with knowledge as the key to profits. Most of the new developments have a technological angle that makes it necessary to really understand what is going on. This is of course true for all sectors of the economy if someone wishes to apply competition law in any meaningful way. Yet, older technologies and the functioning of older business and technology models are better known than those designed in the past few years.

The second issue, the economics issue, is related to this: Most scholars nowadays favor a "more economic approach" to cases and apply an effects-based analysis. The models they use and the tools they have at hand are designed for traditional sectors. Yet, it is a characteristic of this digital economy that it works according to other yardsticks. For example, multi-sided markets and platforms that play a crucial role in many ICT undertakings were not a particularly significant tool in former times. They stand for the integration of companies and their close links to consumers. Now, platforms have been a subject of analysis for a couple of years, and still we are not fully sure how these platforms work and what to make of them. Other economic topics are still under investigation, the attention economy for instance, the power of information or the role of intellectual property rights for dynamic sectors. The troubles with patents hindering innovation instead of incentivizing it started in the ICT sector, not in other branches of the economy. The technology has led to new economic phenomena that are hard for competition officials to decipher. In the investigation of companies like Google, HRS or others mentioned in this book it seems that it took the enforcers a lot of time to understand how the companies really make money. And regarding the outcome of some of these cases, the application of competition law did not necessarily hit the mark.

This is the final issue that shines through in all contributions in this book: the results of competition law investigations are often disappointing. Sometimes it takes far too long to reach conclusions for markets that are reshaped every day. Additionally, the ever more popular commitments in abuse or merger control require a prognosis. Yet, to give a prognosis of such dynamic markets as in the ICT sector amounts to nothing more than reading tea leaves. Ronny Hauck states that the commitments made by Google in the U.S. case were barely enforceable and weak. Simonetta Vezzoso calls for an extra-cautious approach to interventions due to the dynamics of the eBook market. And Pablo Ibàñez Colomo reminds the reader that the purpose of competition law is not to achieve optimal market design but to give firms the ability and incentive to outperform rivals. It is a challenge that competition authorities can hardly master (not to speak of private enforcement)—to intervene in technology-driven markets that are constantly changing. Would it be an alternative to favor a regulation freeze? Probably not, but it is necessary to reconsider the role of prognosis and the rationale for intervention in fast-moving markets. Ex-ante and ex-post evaluation of competitive behavior may come under new scrutiny.

3 Conclusions

What do we make of this picture formed by the distinct contributions in this book? In my view it is necessary to call for a "more technological approach" to competition law.[6] After economics had its fair share, it is time to look to other disciplines that could inform competition law enforcement. In the digital economy, the scholars who need to be addressed are those who know the technology best and who understand the business models that ride on the latest developments.

What would it mean to approach competition law with a technological mode of thinking?

Approaching this question by way of analogy, one could think of the more economic approach: It entailed, (a) a thorough analysis of individual cases with a view to their economic effects, and (b) it favored consumer welfare (which essentially means productive and allocative efficiencies) as a yardstick for the application of competition law. The more technological approach, accordingly, would mean that (a) cases are individually analyzed with a view to the technological effects of the behavior and the decision, and (b) the yardstick for deciding cases would be the openness for future innovation (which essentially means dynamic efficiencies). This, of course, requires an understanding of technologies, business models and the economics of a digital economy that we are still researching. The *Google* case, labelled as the landmark case for the information economy,[7] is a warning sign of the inability to understand what the search engine giant really does and how it works.

---

[6] I owe the term "more technological approach" to my academic mentor Josef Drexl. Cf. *Podszun*, Kartellrecht in der Internet-Branche: Zeit für den more technological approach, WuW 2014, 249.

[7] *Körber*, Google im Fokus des Kartellrechts, WRP 2012, 761.

Five elements may be identified as strategic features of a more technological approach. First and foremost, competition law should embrace the innovation paradigm. While it is textbook wisdom that innovation is a goal of competition law equal to efficiency, it does not really play a vital role in most decisions and is rarely analyzed in economic evidence. The innovation paradigm would mean to check carefully the effects of behavior and decisions on the power to invest and to innovate. Secondly, competition law scholars should acknowledge that a new economic environment needs a new terminology and new concepts. Instead of equating a website to a shop in the city center it would be much more productive to accept that there are new phenomena that have new names. A positive example is the way platform markets are analyzed as a new feature. Thirdly, competition law should acknowledge that it can never be neutral towards different business models. Even though this is a standard claim ("it is up to consumers to decide which channel of distribution to favor") regulation always restricts or promotes certain undertakings and their concepts over others. When deciding on free-riding, for instance in distribution, this is an immanently political decision, not an economic one. Economists and lawyers can only show possible grounds and implications but they cannot decide autonomously. Fourthly, a more technological approach would take a different view of consumers. They are much more involved these days in production processes, giving input as more educated and able customers than ever. Consumers are also more flexible and may develop new preferences very soon with new innovations coming along. Reducing consumers' choice to their current preferences would not be adequate. Finally, competition authorities should refrain from the market design that was inspired by the belief that modern economics allows smart interventions. The very detailed commitments work only in a static environment and may even stabilize this instead of enabling innovation and leap-frog technologies. The innovation paradigm taken seriously would mean to believe again in Hayek's discovery procedure of competition and in Schumpeter's creative destruction. Experiments and failures will be included. If companies like Microsoft or Nokia do not know what happens next—how should bureaucracies in Brussels or other places know?

In 2004, two decisions were taken. In Brussels, the European Commission decided on a fine against Microsoft after an extensive 5-year-investigation. The case, tested in Court until 2007, is regarded as the most important antitrust battle in Europe. In Harvard, a 20-year old student, Mark Zuckerberg, founded a social network called Facebook, together with friends, with very little resources. The reader may wonder which of the two events did more for competition in the ICT sector in the subsequent years. At best, competition law may help to promote technological leaps. It is time for a more technological approach to competition law.